French
Glossary of
Banking and
Finance

French-English
English-French

EuroLexus series

First published in Great Britain in 1995 by
Impact Books
Axe and Bottle Court, 70 Newcomen Street, London SE1 1YT

ISBN 1 874687 46 3

Printed and bound by The Guernsey Press, Guernsey

ont contribué/contributors

Steve Steadman   Catherine Stringer

assistante de rédaction/editorial assistant
Agnès Dionisi

TABLE DES MATIÈRES
CONTENTS

PRÉFACE
PREFACE

Ce lexique contient une grande variété de termes susceptibles d'être utilisés ou rencontrés par quiconque exerce une activité en relation avec le monde de la banque et des finances. Il couvre de nombreux domaines dont ceux des cartes de crédit, chèques, comptes, taux d'intérêt, prêts et crédits, échanges bancaires internationaux, la Bourse, les contrats à terme, le monde du change, les marchés monétaires et les placements. Les annexes proposent un exemple de documents financiers et bancaires français et britanniques (bordereau de remise de chèques, crédit documentaire, traites bancaires, etc.). Autant d'atouts qui font de cet ouvrage un outil de référence fort pratique pour les professionnels et les étudiants du monde de la banque et des finances.

This glossary contains a wide range of vocabulary likely to be used or encountered by those involved in banking or finance. Specific areas dealt with include credit cards, cheques, accounts, interest rates, lending and borrowing, international banking, the Stock Market, futures, options, foreign exchange, money markets and investment. With appendices giving examples of French and English financial and banking documents such a bank giro credit slip, documentary credit, bank drafts and more, this book is a highly practical reference tool for practitioners or students of banking and finance.

*abréviations/***abbreviations**

adj	*adjectif*/adjective
adv	*adverbe*/adverb
Am	American English/*anglais américain*
Br	British English/*anglais britannique*
f	*féminin*/feminine
m	*masculin*/masculine
pl	*pluriel*/plural
qch	*quelque chose*/something
qn	*quelqu'un*/somebody
sb	somebody/*quelqu'un*
sth	something/*quelque chose*
vi	*verbe intransitif*/intransitive verb
vt	*verbe transitif*/transitive verb
≈	*équivalent culturel*/cultural equivalent

A

AAA: notation AAA *f* triple-A rating

abaisser [*taux*] to lower

abandon à l'échéance *m* abandonment at expiry

abandonner à l'échéance to abandon at expiry

abattement *m* [*d'une somme*] allowance

aborder le marché to access the market

absorption *f* takeover

accéder à des financements to have access to finance

acceptation *f* acceptance

accepter un cours acheteur to hit a bid

accord d'atermoiement *m* standstill agreement

accord de clearing *m* clearing agreement

accord de taux futur *m* forward rate agreement

accorder des crédits to grant loans

accrédité *m* beneficiary, payee

accrédité authorized

accréditif *m* credential; [*lettre de crédit*] letter of credit

accroître une position to increase a position

achat *m* purchase

achat ferme *m* bought deal

achat à crédit *m* purchase on credit, credit purchase

achat à terme *m* forward purchase

achat au comptant *m* cash purchase

achat en bloc *m* block trade

acheminement des données *m* data routing

acheter to buy, to purchase

acheter à crédit to buy on credit

acheter à terme to buy forward

acheter au comptant to buy for cash

acheteur *m* buyer, purchaser

acompte *m* down payment, payment on account; [*versement*] instalment

acompte mensuel *m* monthly instalment, monthly payment

acompte sur dividende *m* interim dividend

acquisition *f* acquisition

acquit *m* receipt; *pour acquit* payment received, received with thanks

acquit de paiement *m* receipt

acquittement *m* [*de facture*] payment

acquitter [*facture*] to pay; [*considérer pour acquit*] to receipt

acquitter un premium to pay a premium

acte *m* deed

acte commercial *m* commercial deed

acte hypothécaire *m* mortgage deed

acte notarié *m* notarized deed

acte de cession *m* deed of transfer, certificate of transfer

acte de propriété *m* title deed

acte de vente *m* deed of sale

acteur de marché *m* market player

acteurs du système financier *mpl* players in the financial system

actif *m* [*bancaire*] credit balance; [*de société*] asset; assets

actif circulant *m* current assets

actif corporel *m* tangible asset

actif fictif *m* fictitious asset

actif financier *m* financial asset

actif illiquide *m* non-liquid asset

actif immobilisé *m* fixed asset

actif incorporel *m* intangible asset

actif liquide *m* liquid asset

actif monétaire *m* monetary asset

actif net *m* net assets, net worth

actif sous-jacent *m* underlying asset

actif soustractif *m* depreciated credit balance

actif stable *m* fixed asset, long-term asset

actif support *m* underlying asset

actif de taux *m* fixed income asset

actif du bilan *m* assets

actifs facilement mobilisables *mpl* easily realizable assets

actifs immobiliers *mpl* property assets

action *f* share; [*juridique*] action, legal action

action convertible *f* convertible share

action gratuite *f* bonus share

action nominative *f* registered share

action non libérée *f* unpaid-up share

action ordinaire *f* ordinary share

action privilégiée *f* preference share, preferred share *Am*

action spécifique *f* golden share

action à dividende prioritaire *f* preference share

action à droit de vote double *f* share with double voting right

action au porteur *f* bearer share

action de croissance *f* growth stock

action de jouissance *f* dividend share

action de priorité *f* preference share, preferred share *Am*

actions à fort rendement *fpl* income stock

actionnaire *mf* shareholder

actionnariat *m* [*actionnaires*] shareholders; [*détention d'actions*] share ownership

actionnement de la garantie *m* exercise of the guarantee

actions *fpl* shares, stock *Am*; *avoir des actions dans* to have a shareholding in, to have shares in; *détenir des actions d'une société* to hold shares in a company

actions détenues *fpl* shares held

actions libérées *fpl* paid-up share capital

activité bancaire *f* banking business

activité crédit *f* credit activity

activités de marché *fpl* market activities

activités sur des niches *fpl* niche activities

actuaire *mf* actuary

actualisation *f* update;

[*comptabilité*] calculation of net present value

actualiser to update; [*couverture*] to mark to market

actuariel actuarial

adhérent-compensateur *m* clearing member

administrateur indépendant de la gestion *m* non-executive director

administrateur judiciaire *m* receiver

administration des titres *f* securities department

admission à la cote *f* admission to the Stock Exchange List

ADP (= Action à Dividende Prioritaire) *f* preference share

AFB (= Association Française de Banque) French bankers' association

affacturage *m* factoring

affaires *fpl* business

affaissement *m* slump

affecter des fonds à to allocate funds to

afficher des conditions to attach conditions

affilié affiliated

affirmation de créance *f* proof of debt, statement of claim

AFPER (= Association Française des Porteurs d'Emprunts Russes) *f* French association of Russian bondholders

agence *f* agency; [*d'une banque*] branch

agence bancaire *f* bank branch

agence de notation *f* rating agency

agence de rating *f* rating agency

agence de notation financière *f* rating agency

agent de change *m* stockbroker, broker

agio *m* charge

agios bancaires *mpl* bank charges

agrégat monétaire *m* monetary aggregate

agrément *m* authorization

agrément en qualité de banque *m* recognition as a bank

AID (= Association Internationale de Développement) *f* IDA

aide-comptable *mf* assistant accountant, accounts clerk

aide financière *f* financial aid

ajustement *m* adjustment

aléa des taux d'intérêt *m* interest rate risk

aléatoire risky

alimenter un compte to pay money into an account

alléger le risque to reduce the risk

allocataire *mf* recipient, beneficiary

allocation *f* [*des fonds*] allocation, distribution

allouer to allocate

amorti [*bien*] depreciated; [*capital*] amortized

amortir [*frais, coût*] to amortize, to write off

amortir une dette [*emprunteur*] to pay off a debt, to amortize a debt; [*prêteur*] to write off a debt

amortissable redeemable

amortissement *m* [*de crédit, de dette*] redemption, paying off, amortization; [*par prêteur*] write-off; [*dépréciation*] depreciation

amortissement anticipé *m* early redemption

amortissement dégressif *m* accelerated depreciation

amortissement-dépenses *m* amortization of expenditure, write-off of expenditure

amortissement dérogatoire *m* excess tax depreciation over normal depreciation

amortissement in fine *m* bullet repayment

amortissement linéaire *m* straightline depreciation

amortissements cumulés *mpl* cumulative depreciation

amortissements différés *mpl* deferred depreciation

amputer [*une valeur*] to reduce

an: par an per year

analyse Chartiste *f* chartism

analyse des comptes *f* accounts analysis

analyse des données *f* data analysis

analyste *mf* analyst

analyste graphique *mf* chartist

ANJB (= Association Nationale des Juristes de Banque) *f* national association of banking lawyers

année budgétaire *f* financial year, fiscal year *Am*

année civile *f* calendar year

année comptable *f* accounting year, fiscal year *Am*

année fiscale *f* financial year, fiscal year *Am*

annuité *f* [*rente*] annuity

annuité constante *f* fixed annual payment

annuité d'amortissement *f* annual depreciation, annual writedown

anticipation *f* advance

anticipé [*remboursement de dette*] early

anticiper un paiement to pay in advance

antidater to backdate; [*contrat*] to antedate

anti-inflationniste anti-inflation(ary)

appel *m* call

appel au marché *m* market call

appel de couverture *m* margin call

appel de garantie *m* margin call

appel de marge *m* margin call

application *f* cross trade

apporter en caution to provide as surety, to provide as collateral

apposer sa signature to affix one's signature

appréciation du franc contre le mark *f* appreciation of the franc against the mark

approvisionner un compte to replenish an account, to pay money into an account

apurement *m* [*de comptes*] auditing

apurer [*comptes*] to audit

apurer une dette to discharge a debt

arbitrage *m* arbitrage, arbitraging

arbitrage des taux d'intérêt *m* interest rate arbitrage

arbitragiste *m* arbitrageur

argent *m* money; [*métal*] silver

argent comptant *m* cash

argent liquide *m* cash

argent à trois mois *m* three-month money

argent au jour le jour *m* overnight money, call money

argent de gré à gré entre banques *m* interbank money

arrérages *mpl* back interest, arrears

arrêt de paiement *m* stoppage of payment(s)

arrêté de compte *m* closing off of an account, settlement of an account

arrêter un compte to close (off) an account, to settle an account

arrêter un marché to close a deal

arriver à échéance to fall due; [*bail*] to expire; [*prêt*] to mature

arriver à expiration [*carte bancaire*] to reach the expiry date

arrondir to round off

assemblée annuelle *f* annual (general) meeting

assemblée générale *f* annual general meeting, AGM

assemblée des actionnaires *f* shareholders' meeting

assignation *f* assignment

assignation par tirage au sort *f* random assignment

association bancaire *f* banking association

Association française de banque *f* French Bankers' Association

Association française des porteurs d'emprunts russes *f* French association of Russian bondholders

Association française des sociétés de Bourse *f* French association of Securities Houses

Association nationale des juristes de banque *f* national association of banking lawyers

assumer les frais to bear the costs

assumer un risque to take on a risk

assurance auto *f* car insurance

assurance dommages *f* property insurance

assurance-vie *f* life insurance

assurance d'un prix *f* guaranteeing of a price

assurance de risques *f* risk insurance

assurance des cartes de crédit *f* credit card insurance

assureur *m* insurer

assurfinance *f* insurance-related savings products

atermoiement *m* standstill

ATF (= Accord de Taux Futur) *m* FRA

attaquant *m* corporate raider

attestation de rejet *f* [*de chèque*] notification of returned cheque

attribuer [*des actions*] to allot

attribut financier *m* financial attribute

attribution *f* [*d'actions*] allotment

audit interne *m* internal audit

auditeur *m* auditor

augmentation de capital *f* increase in capital

augmentation des revenus *f* increase in revenues

autocouverture *f* natural hedging

autofinancé financed from cashflow

autofinancement *m* financing from cashflow, cashflow

automate (bancaire) *m* cash machine

automatisation *f* automation

automatiser to automate

automatisme bancaire *m* automated banking

autorisation de prélèvement *f* direct debit mandate

autorité réglementaire *f* regulatory authority

aval: pour aval guaranteed by

aval bancaire *m* bank guarantee, aval

avaler une carte [*distributeur automatique*] to eat a card
avaliser to avalize
avaliste *m* guarantor
avance (de fonds) *f* advance
avance en compte débiteur *f* overdraft
avance en devises *f* currency advance
avance sur recettes *f* advance against income
avance sur titres *f* securities-backed loan
avantage concurrentiel *m* competitive advantage
avis *m* notification; [*document*] advice, notice, note
avis d'exécution *m* contract note
avis d'exercice *m* exercise notice
avis d'opération sur titre *m* contract note
avis de crédit *m* credit advice
avis de débit *m* debit advice
avis de levée *m* exercise notice
avis de paiement *m* payment advice

avis de prélèvement *m* debit advice
avis de prélèvement automatique *m* direct debit advice
avis de réception de fonds *m* credit advice
avis de rejet *m* [*de chèque*] notice of returned cheque
avis de sort *m* advice note
avis de virement *m* (bank) transfer advice
avis de la banque *m* bank notification, bank advice
aviser to inform, to advise
avoir *m* [*de société*] assets; [*capital*] capital; [*sur compte*] credit; [*note de crédit*] credit note
avoir-client *m* customer credit
avoir fiscal *m* tax credit
avoir de compte *m* account credit
avoir en banque *m* bank credit
avoir en devises *m* foreign currency holding
avoirs en or *mpl* gold assets
ayant-compte *m* account holder

B

back-office *m* back office
bail emphytéotique *m* long lease
bail financier *m* finance lease

bail d'exploitation *m* operating lease
bailleur *m* lessor

bailleur de fonds *m* backer

baisse sensible (des cours) *f* sharp fall (in prices)

baissier bear, bearish

balance *f* balance

balance créditrice *f* credit balance

balance de vérification *f* trial balance

balance des paiements *f* balance of payments

bancaire banking, bank; *informatique bancaire* computerized banking

bancarisation: *la bancarisation de l'économie* the growing role of banks in the economy; *la bancarisation des ménages* the growing relationship between households and banks

bancarisé with a bank account; *une clientèle qui n'est pas totalement bancarisée* a customer base not all of which has a bank connection

bancassurance *f* bancassurance

bancassureur *m* insurance banker

bancatique *f* electronic banking, on-line banking

banque *f* bank; [*activité, profession*] banking

banque AFB *f* AFB-affiliated bank

banque agréée *f* recognized bank

banque centrale *f* central bank

banque centrale européenne *f* European central bank

banque commerciale *f* commercial bank, joint-stock bank; [*activité*] commercial banking

banque compensatrice *f* clearing bank

banque confirmatrice *f* confirming bank

banque coopérative *f* cooperative bank

banque correspondante *f* correspondent bank

banque dépositaire *f* custodian bank

banque électronique *f* electronic banking

Banque européenne d'investissement *f* European Investment Bank

banque généraliste *f* generalized bank

banque inscrite *f* registered bank

banque libre-service *f* self-service bank; [*activité*] self-service banking

banque mandataire *f* agent bank

Banque Mondiale *f* World Bank

banque mutualiste *f* cooperative bank, mutual bank

Banque nationale de Belgique *f* National Bank of Belgium

banque notificatrice *f* advising bank

banque off shore *f* offshore bank

banque populaire *f* high street bank *Br*

banque postale *f* = Girobank

banque privée *f* private bank; [*activité*] private banking

banque toute informatique *f* totally computerized banking

banque universelle *f* full-service bank, universal bank; [*activité*] global banking

banque à distance *f* direct banking

banque à domicile *f* home banking

banque à réseau *f* high street bank *Br*

banque d'affaires *f* merchant bank *Br*, investment bank

Banque d'Angleterre *f* Bank of England

banque d'émission *f* issuing bank

banque d'entreprise *f* corporate banking

banque d'épargne *f* savings bank

banque de crédit *f* credit bank

banque de crédit à long terme *f* long-term credit bank

banque de crédit à moyen terme *f* medium-term credit bank

banque de dépôts *f* clearing bank, high street bank *Br*

banque de détail *f* retail bank; [*activité*] retail banking

Banque de France *f* Bank of France

banque de gestion de patrimoine *f* trust bank

banque de gros *f* wholesale bank; [*activité*] wholesale banking

banque de placement *f* issuing house

Banque de Règlements Internationaux *f* Bank for International Settlements

banqueroute *f* bankruptcy

banquier *m* banker

banquier actionnaire *m* shareholding bank

banquier central *m* central banker

banquier prêteur *m* lending bank

banquier d'affaires *m* merchant banker *Br*, investment banker

barrer un chèque to cross a cheque

barrière réglementaire *f* regulatory barrier

barrières antiraid *fpl* antiraid precautions

base *f* basis; *à base d'actions* equity-based

base monétaire *f* monetary base

base de clientèle *f* client base

BEI (= **Banque Européenne d'Investissement**) *f* EIB

bénéfice *m* profit

bénéfice brut d'exploitation *m* gross operating profit

bénéfice net *m* net profit

bénéfice par action *m* earnings per share

bénéficiaire *mf* beneficiary, payee

BERD (= **Banque Européenne pour la Reconstruction et le Développement**) *f* EBRD

BFR (= **Besoin en Fonds de Roulement**) *m* working capital requirement

bien hypothéqué *m* mortgaged property

bien immobilier *m* real estate

bien mobilier *m* personal estate

biens immobiliers *mpl* property assets

bilan *m* balance sheet

bilan bancaire *m* bank balance sheet

bilan comptable *m* balance sheet

bilan condensé *m* summary balance sheet

bilan financier *m* financial statement

bilan intérimaire *m* interim statement

bilan simplifié *m* simplified balance sheet

bilan de prévoyance *m* forecast balance sheet

bilantiel balance-sheet

billet vert *m* [*dollar*] greenback

billet à ordre *m* promissory note

billet de banque *m* bank note, bank bill *Am*

billet de trésorerie *m* commercial paper

billets en circulation *mpl* notes in circulation

blanchiment de l'argent *m* money laundering

bloc *m* block of shares

bloc de contrôle *m* controlling interest

blocage *m* blocking; [*d'un compte*] escrow; [*de prix, salaires*] freezing

bloquer [*des fonds*] to block, to freeze

blue book *m* blue book

BMTN (= Bon à Moyen Terme Négociable) *m* medium-term negotiable note

bon *m* voucher, slip, coupon

bon à moyen terme négociable *m* medium-term negotiable note

bon d'épargne *m* savings certificate

bon de caisse *m* interest-bearing note; [*justifiant sortie de fonds*] cash voucher

bon de souscription d'actions *m* share warrant

bon du Trésor *m* Treasury bill, Treasury bond, Treasury note

bon pour aval guaranteed by

bonification *f* [*de crédit, etc.*] subsidization

bons de capitalisation *mpl* savings bonds

boom *m* boom

bordereau *m* [*formulaire*] form; [*liste*] list

bordereau d'escompte *m* list of bills for discount

bordereau d'exécution *m* order execution slip

bordereau d'opération *m* paying-in slip

bordereau de caisse *m* cash statement

bordereau de compte *m* statement of account

bordereau de crédit *m* credit note

bordereau de remboursement *m* withdrawal slip

bordereau de remise (d'espèces) *m* paying-in slip

bordereau de remise de chèques *m* paying-in slip

bordereau de vente *m* sales contract

bordereau de versement (d'espèces) *m* paying-in slip

borne basse *f* lower limit

borne haute *f* upper limit

boucler une position to close (out) a position

Bourse *f* Stock Exchange, Stock Market; [*jour de Bourse*] trading day; *après Bourse* after market; *avant Bourse* before hours

Bourse coulisse *f* unlisted market

Bourse internationale *f* international exchange

Bourse régionale *f* regional exchange

Bourse de commerce *f* commodities exchange

Bourse des valeurs *f* Stock Exchange

boursicoter to dabble on the Stock Market

boursicoteur *m* dabbler on the Stock Market

boursier Stock Exchange, Stock Market, market

BPF (= Bon Pour Francs) good for ... francs

brader to sell off cheaply

BRI (= Banque de Règlements Internationaux) *f* BIS

brut gross

9

bulle (financière) *f* (financial) bubble

bulletin de commande *m* order form

bulletin de versement *m* paying-in slip, paying-in form

bulletin de salaire *m* payslip, salary slip

bulletin de souscription d'actions *m* share subscription form

bureau de change *m* bureau de change

but: *à but lucratif* profit-making; *à but non lucratif* non-profit-making, not-for-profit *Am*

C

CA (= Chiffre d'Affaires) *m* turnover

cabinet financier *m* financial firm

cabinet d'experts financiers *m* firm of financial experts

CAC 40 (= Cotation Assistée en Continu) *m* ≈ FTSE 100

cadre réglementaire *m* regulatory framework

caisse *f* [*liquide*] cash; [*guichet*] cashdesk

caisse nationale *f* national savings bank

caisse régionale *f* regional savings bank

caisse d'épargne *f* savings bank

caisse d'épargne-logement *f* building society *Br*, savings and loan association *Am*, S&L *Am*

caisse d'épargne et de prévoyance *f* savings and providential institution

caisse de garantie *f* credit guarantee institution

caisse de retraite *f* pension fund

caisse de retraite complémentaire *f* supplementary pension fund

Caisse des Dépôts et Consignations *f* = public institution responsible for some deposits and funds in escrow

calendrier des émissions *m* timetable of issues

call *m* call (option)

call couvert *m* covered call

call francs put dollars *m* call francs put dollars

cambiste *mf* money trader, foreign exchange dealer, currency dealer

camoufler le bilan to window-dress the accounts

capacité à emprunter *f* borrowing capacity

capacité d'achat *f* purchasing power

capacité d'endettement *f* borrowing capacity

capacité de financement *f* financing capacity

capital *m* capital; [*par contraste à l'intérêt*] capital, principal; *détenir 5% du capital de* to hold 5% of the shares in, to have a 5% shareholding in

capital appelé *m* called-up capital

capital-développement *m* development capital

capital engagé *m* capital employed

capital fixe *m* fixed capital

capital flottant *m* floating capital

capital improductif *m* idle capital, unproductive capital

capital initial *m* initial capital, start-up capital

capital-investissement *m* investment capital

capital-investissement d'État *m* State investment capital

capital nominal *m* nominal capital

capital non appelé *m* uncalled capital

capital remplacement *m* replacement capital

capital-risque *m* venture capital

capital roulant *m* working capital

capital social *m* share capital, issued (share) capital

capital souscrit *m* subscribed capital

capital souscrit et appelé *m* called-up subscribed capital

capital souscrit et appelé, non versé *m* subscribed capital called and unpaid

capital souscrit non appelé *m* uncalled subscribed capital

capital transmission *m* transfer capital

capital versé *m* paid-up share capital

capital de départ *m* start-up capital

capital de réserve *m* reserve capital

capital de roulement *m* working capital

capitalisation *f* capitalization

capitalisation boursière *f* market capitalization

capitalisation unitaire *f* unit capitalization

capitalisation viagère *f* life capitalization

capitaliser to capitalize

capitaux *mpl* capital

capitaux disponibles *mpl* available capital

capitaux fébriles *mpl* hot money

capitaux permanents *mpl* long-term capital

capitaux propres *mpl* equity (capital), shareholders' equity, shareholders' funds

carnet d'épargne *m* passbook, savings book

carnet d'ordres public *m* public order book

carnet de chèques *m* chequebook *Br*, checkbook *Am*

carte *f* card

carte accréditive *f* credit card; [*de magasin*] charge card

carte bancaire *f* banker's card

carte bancaire de paiement national *f* national payment card

Carte Bleue (Visa®) *f* Visa® card

11

carte libre-service bancaire *f* cashpoint card

carte monoprestataire *f* single-function card

carte patrimoine *f* asset card

carte prépayée *f* prepaid card

carte prépayée multiprestataire *f* multifunction prepaid card

carte privative *f* store card, charge card

carte-ville *f* local payment card

carte à mémoire *f* smart card

carte à puce *f* smart card

carte de crédit *f* credit card

carte de débit *f* debit card

carte de paiement *f* payment card, debit card

carte de retrait (d'espèces) *f* cash card, cashpoint card

caution *f* guarantee, surety, security; *être caution personnelle de* to stand surety for; *en caution* as surety

caution de banque *f* bank guarantee

caution de bonne fin *f* performance bond

cautionnement *m* guarantee

cautionnement solidaire *m* joint and several guarantee

cautionner to secure, to guarantee

CB (= Carte Bancaire) credit card

CB (= Carte Bleue®) Visa®

C/C (= Compte (de) Chèque) *m* C/A

CCB (= Compte de Chèque Bancaire) *m* C/A

CCP (= Compte Chèque Postal) *m* post office giro account

CCP (= Compte Courant Postal) *m* post office giro account

CD (= Certificat de Dépôt) *m* CD

CD à taux flottant *m* FRCD, floating-rate CD

CDN (= Certificat de Dépôt Négociable) *m* negotiable CD

CEA (= Compte d'Épargne en Actions) *m* PEP

Cec (= Centre d'Échange des opérations à Compensation) *m* [*en Belgique*] central clearing house

CEDEL (= CEntrale DE Livraison de valeurs mobilières) *f* CEDEL, Eurobonds clearing house in Luxembourg

céder [*des actions*] to transfer

céder des fonds to supply funds

Cenb (= Comité Européen de Normalisation Bancaire) *m* European Banking Standards Committee

Cencep (= CEntre National des Caisses d'Épargne et de Prévoyance) *m* central body for savings and providential institutions

centaine *f* hundred

centrale d'incidences de paiements *f* register of unpaid trade bills

Centre national des caisses d'épargne et de prévoyance *m* central body for savings and providential institutions

centre d'opposition *m* [*vol de CB*] lost and stolen card office

CEPME (= Crédit d'Équipement des Petites et Moyennes Entreprises) *m* specialist body for lending to small and medium-sized businesses

certificat d'actions *m* share certificate

certificat d'investissement *m*

certificate of investment

certificat de dépôt *m* certificate of deposit

certificat de dépôt négociable *m* negotiable certificate of deposit

certificat de dépôt à taux flottant *m* floating rate certificate of deposit

certificat de dépôt à taux révisable *m* floating rate certificate of deposit

certificat de non-paiement *m* [*de chèque*] notification of unpaid cheque; [*de lettre de change*] certificate of dishonour

certificat de titres *m* share certificate, securities certificate

certificats d'investissement *mpl* shares without voting rights, non-voting stock

certificats de dépôts négociables *mpl* tradeable certificates of deposit

certifié attested

cessation d'activité *f* ceasing of trading

cessation de paiement *f* suspension of payments

cessible transferable

cession *f* [*d'actions*] transfer, assignment

cession-bail *f* sale and leaseback

cessionnaire *mf* transferee, assignee

Cfonb (= **Comité Français d'Organisation et de Normalisation Bancaires**) *m* French committe for banking organization and standardization

CH No (= **chèque numéro**) cheque No.

chambre d'enregistrement *f* registration body

chambre de compensation *f* clearing house

chambre de compensation automatisée *f* automated clearing house, ACH

change *m* foreign exchange

change à terme *m* forward exchange

charge: être à la charge de [*appel, etc.*] to be chargeable to

charge à payer *f* sum payable

charge d'intérêt *f* interest charge

chargé de clientèle *m* account executive

chargé de clientèle grand public *m* personal account manager

chargé de compte *m* account manager

charges d'exploitation *fpl* operating expenses

charges financières *fpl* interest and other finance charges

chef comptable *m* chief accountant

chef de file *m* lead manager

chèque *m* cheque *Br*, check *Am*

chèque bancaire *m* bank cheque, cashier's check *Am*

chèque barré *m* crossed cheque

chèque bloqué *m* blocked cheque

chèque certifié *m* certified cheque

chèque compensé *m* cleared cheque

chèque nominatif *m* cheque made out to name

chèque postal *m* post office cheque

chèque retourné *m* returned cheque

13

chèque au porteur *m* cheque made out to bearer, bearer cheque

chèque d'entreprise *m* company cheque

chèque de banque *m* banker's draft, cashier's check *Am*

chèque de virement *m* transfer cheque

chèque en blanc *m* blank cheque

chèque en bois *m* cheque which bounces, rubber cheque

chèque non crédité *m* uncleared cheque

chèque non endossable *m* non-negotiable cheque

chèque sans provision *m* uncovered cheque, cheque that bounces

chèques en circulation *mpl* outstanding cheques

chéquier *m* chequebook *Br*, checkbook *Am*

chevalier blanc *m* white knight

chevalier noir *m* black knight

chiffrage *m* adding up, totalling

chiffre *m* figure; *en chiffres* [*montant*] in figures

chiffre d'affaires *m* turnover

se **chiffrer à** to add up to, to total

chiffreur *m* payments coding clerk

choc boursier *m* market crisis

chroniquier boursier *m* market commentator

chute ample *f* freefall

chute brutale *f* sharp fall

chute brutale des cours *f* sharp drop in rates

chute des cours *f* fall in prices

circuit financier *m* financial circulation

circuit de recouvrement *m* collection process

circuits financiers *mpl* financial circulation

circuits de financement *mpl* circulation of finance

circulation monétaire *f* circulation of money

circulation des capitaux *f* circulation of capital

circulation des devises *f* circulation of currency

circulation des flux *f* circulation of funds

Ciri (= Centre Interbancaire de Recherche Informatique) *m* [*en Belgique*] Ciri

clause pari passu *f* pari passu clause

clause pénale *f* penalty clause

clause au porteur *f* pay to bearer clause

clause d'annulation *f* cancellation clause

clause de réserve de propriété *f* retention of title clause

clause de résiliation *f* termination clause, cancellation clause

client commercial *m* commercial customer

client douteux *m* doubtful debtor, doubtful debt

clientèle *f* customer base, customers, clientele

clientèle bancaire *f* banking customers, bank customers

clignotants économiques *mpl* economic indicators

cliquet: à cliquet lock-in

clore un compte to close an account

clore une position to close (out) a position

clore une position en partie to partially close (out) a position

clore une position en totalité to totally close (out) a position

clôture *f* [*de la Bourse*] close; *en clôture* at market close, at the close

clôture annuelle des livres *f* year-end closing of accounts

clôture d'une position *f* closing (out) of a position

clôture de compte *f* closing of account

clôture de l'exercice *f* end of the financial year

clôture de la Bourse *f* Stock Exchange close

clôture du marché *f* closing of the market, market close

clôture par rachat *f* closure by repurchase

clôturer to close; *clôturer un compte* to close an account

clôturer à perte to close at a loss

club d'épargne *m* savings club

club des amis *m* fan club

Cncb (= Centre National Cartes Bleues) *m* national credit card centre

CNCC (= Compagnie Nationale des Commissaires aux Comptes) *f* national auditors' society

COB (= Commission des Opérations de Bourse) *f* Paris Stock Exchange watchdog, ≈ SIB *Br*, SEC *Am*

code *m* code; [*de carte bancaire*] PIN, PIN number

code banque *m* bank sort code

code client *m* customer code, customer reference number

code confidentiel *m* private code; [*de carte bancaire*] PIN

code guichet *m* bank branch code

code de bonne conduite *m* code of conduct

code des assurances *m* insurance code

codébiteur *m* joint debtor

codétenteur *m* joint holder

CODEVI (= COmpte pour le DÉVeloppement Industriel) *m* industrial development savings account, tax-free deposit account

coefficient d'exploitation *m* performance ratio, operating ratio

coefficient de couverture *m* capital adequacy ratio

coefficient de fonds propres et de ressources permanentes *m* capital adequacy ratio

coefficient de liquidité *m* liquidity ratio

coefficient de solvabilité *m* risk asset ratio

co-emprunteur *m* co-borrower

coffre de nuit *m* night safe

collatéralisation *f* collateralization

collecte brute *f* gross revenue

collecte nette *f* net revenue

collecte de capitaux *f* capital revenue

collecter des dépôts to take deposits

colonne créditrice *f* credit column

colonne débitrice *f* debit column

combinaison de positions *f* combination of positions

combler [*déficit, perte*] to make good

comité consultatif d'actionnaires *m* shareholder consultative committee

comité d'audit *m* audit committee

comité de crédit *m* credit committee

Comité de la réglementation bancaire *m* Banking regulation committee

commandement à payer *m* order to pay, summons to pay

commerçant "Cartes Bancaires" *m* establishment accepting credit cards

commerce *m* trade, commerce

commerce d'échange *m* countertrade

commercer to trade

commercial commercial, business; [*embargo, tribunal*] trade

commettant *m* principal

commis principal *m* senior clerk

commis de banque *m* bank clerk

commission *f* commission

commission bancaire *f* bank commission, bank charge, bank fee

Commission bancaire *f* Bank Regulatory Body, Banking Commission

commission d'acceptation *f* acceptance fee

commission d'assurance *f* insurance commission

commission d'encaissement *f* collection charge, collection fee

commission d'endos *f* endorsement commission, endorsement fee

commission d'engagement *f* commitment fee

commission de change *f* exchange commission

commission de compte *f* account commission, account fee

commission de confirmation *f* confirmation fee, confirmation commission; [*pour crédit*] facility fee

commission de courtage *f* brokerage fee

commission de garantie *f* guarantee commission, underwriting fee

commission de gestion *f* [*d'une sicav*] management fee

commission de mouvement *f* transaction charge

commission de paiement *f* collection charge, collection fee

commission de service *f* service charge

commission de tenue de compte *f* account handling fee

commission de vente *f* sales commission

Commission des opérations de Bourse *f* Paris Stock Exchange watchdog

commission sur le plus fort découvert mensuel *f* bank charge based on the highest overdraft level in a month

commissionnement *m* paying of commission

compagnie d'assurance *f* insurance company

compensable à to be cleared at

compensation *f* [*de chèque*] clearing; [*au marché des changes*] netting

compensation électronique *f* electronic clearing

compenser to clear

compenser une perte to offset a loss

compétition interbancaire *f* interbank competition

complément de retraite *m* pension supplement

compression de crédit *f* credit squeeze

comptabilisation f entering into the accounts; [*dénombrement*] counting

comptabilisation au prix de marché f marking to market

comptabiliser to record in the accounts, to enter in the accounts

comptabiliser au prix de marché to mark to market

comptabiliser des opérations to record transactions

comptabilité f accounts; [*discipline*] accountancy; [*système*] accounting

comptabilité bancaire f bank accounting

comptabilité générale f general accounts; [*système*] financial accounting

comptabilité-gestion financière f financial management accounting

comptabilité de banque f bank accountancy

comptable mf accountant

comptant m cash, spot; *au comptant* [*achat*] cash; [*acheter*] for cash; *cours au comptant* spot price

compte m account; *avoir un compte en banque* to have a bank account; *mettez cela sur mon compte* charge it to my account

compte bancaire m bank account

compte bloqué m escrow account, frozen account

compte centralisateur m central account

compte chèque m current account *Br*, checking account *Am*

compte chèque postal m post office cheque account, giro account

compte client m customer account; [*comptabilité*] account receivable, trade debtor

compte collectif m adjustment account, summary account

compte courant m current account *Br*, checking account *Am*

compte courant bancaire m current account with a bank

compte courant bloqué m escrow current account

compte courant postal m giro account

compte créditeur m [*compte payable*] account payable; [*à la banque*] credit account, account in credit, credit balance

compte débiteur m account receivable; [*à la banque*] debit account, account in debit, overdrawn account, debit balance

compte divisionnaire m divisional account

compte épargne logement m building society account *Br*, savings and loan association account *Am*

compte fiduciaire m fiduciary account

compte joint m joint account

compte loro m vostro account

compte multidevises m multicurrency account

compte nostro m nostro account

compte postal m post office account

compte rémunéré m interest-bearing account

compte-titres m share account

compte vostre m vostro account

compte à découvert *m* overdrawn account

compte à demi *m* joint account

compte à terme *m* forward account

compte à vue *m* demand deposit account

compte d'attente *m* suspense account

compte d'épargne *m* savings account, deposit account

compte d'épargne-retraite *m* retirement savings account

compte d'épargne à régime spécial *m* specialized savings account

compte d'épargne en actions *m* equity savings account, personal equity plan, PEP

compte d'épargne pour le développement industriel *m* industrial development savings account, tax-free deposit account

compte de chèque bancaire *m* current account *Br*, checking account *Am*

compte de compensation *m* clearing account

compte de correspondant *m* correspondent bank account

compte de dépôt *m* deposit account

compte de règlement *m* settlement account

compte de réserve *m* reserve account

compte en banque *m* bank account

compte en devises étrangères *m* foreign currency account

compte sans mouvement *m* dormant account

compte sous mandat de gestion *m* discretionary account

compte sur livret *m* deposit account

comptoir d'escompte *m* discount house

conclure un marché to strike a deal.

conclusion d'un contrat *f* signing of a contract

concours *m* lending, loans outstanding

concours bancaire *m* bank lending

concours à l'exportation *m* export lending, export loans

concours à la clientèle *m* customer lending, customer loans

conditions d'admission à la cote *fpl* listing requirements

conditions d'exécution *fpl* conditions of execution

conditions de banque *fpl* banking terms

conditions de marché *fpl* market conditions

conditions de paiement *fpl* terms (and conditions) of payment

confirmation d'exécution *f* confirmation of execution

confirmation de commande *f* confirmation of order

conjoncture boursière *f* market trend

Conseil national du crédit *m* National Credit Council

conseil patrimonial *m* investment advice, investment consultancy

Conseil des Bourses de Valeurs *m* Paris Bourse regulatory body, Stock Exchange regulatory body

conseiller assurances *m* insurance adviser

conseiller financier *m* financial
adviser, financial consultant

conseiller patrimonial *m*
investment adviser

consentir un prêt to grant a loan

conservateur *m* custodian

conservateur des hypothèques *m*
registrar of mortgages

conservation des titres *f* custody
of shares

consigner une somme to deposit a
sum of money

consolidation de dette *f* debt
consolidation

consolider une dette to
consolidate a debt

consolidés *mpl* consols

**consommation nourrie par le
crédit** *f* credit-driven consumer
spending

consommation des ménages *f*
household consumer spending

consortium de banques *m*
banking consortium

constater une perte to incur a loss

constituer une couverture to
create a hedge

constituer une hypothèque to
create a mortgage

constitution d'hypothèque *f*
creation of a mortgage

constitution de rente *f* annuity
purchase

consumériste consumerist

contact client *m* customer contact

contact clientèle *m* customer
contact

contingentement (de) *m* fixing of
quotas (on)

contracter des dettes to incur
debts, to contract debts

contracter des engagements to
enter into commitments

contracter un crédit to take out a
loan

contraction *f* shrinking

contraction des marges *f*
narrowing of margins

contrat *m* contract

contrat notionnel *m* notional
contract

contrat à terme *m* future, futures
contract

**contrat à terme à échéance
éloignée** *m* deferred future

**contrat à terme sur taux
d'intérêts** *m* interest rate future

contrat à terme sur l'eurodollar
m Eurodollar future

contrat d'animation *m* high-
turnover contract

contrat d'assurance *m* insurance
policy

contrat d'options *m* options
contract

contrat de bail *m* lease contract

contrat de couverture à terme *m*
forward contract

contrat de crédit-bail *m* lease-
purchase contract

contrat de prêt *m* loan agreement

**contrat de retraite par
capitalisation** *m* funded pension
scheme

contrat de swap de devises *m*
currency swap

contrat de swap de taux d'intérêt
m interest rate swap

**contrecarrer les mouvements
spéculatifs** to thwart speculation

contre-garantie *f* counter-
guarantee

contremarque *f* numbered
account

contrepartie *f* counterparty; [*aux
obligations d'une caution*]

consideration; *en contrepartie* as counterparty

contrepartiste *mf* dealer

contresigner to countersign

contrevaleur *f* countervalue

contrôle *m* [*de document*] check; [*de comptes*] audit

contrôle bancaire *m* banking controls

contrôle interne *m* internal auditing

contrôle de solvabilité *m* credit control

contrôle des capitaux *m* capital control

contrôle des changes *m* exchange controls

contrôle des risques *m* risk control

contrôler [*surveiller*] to monitor; [*comptes*] to audit

contrôleur *m* auditor

contrôleur financier *m* financial controller

contrôleur du crédit *m* credit controller

conversion d'un emprunt *f* conversion of loan notes, conversion of loan stock

conversion de créances en actions *f* debt/equity swap, debt-for-equity swap

convertibilité *f* convertibility

convertible convertible

convertir des valeurs to convert securities

convertir un emprunt to convert loan notes, to convert loan stock

convoyer [*des fonds*] to transport by armed guard

convoyeur de fonds *m* armed security escort

corbeille: la corbeille [*Bourse*] the trading floor, the ring, the pit

cosignataire *mf* co-signatory

cotation *f* quotation, quote; *la cotation des actions X était suspendue* trading in X was suspended

cotation (à une bourse) *f* quotation (on an exchange)

cotation assistée en continu *f* continuous automated trading system

cotation à terme *f* forward quotation

cotation à vue *f* spot quotation

cote *f* [*en Bourse*] quotation; [*cote officielle, etc.*] list

cote officielle *f* official list

cote de clôture *f* closing price

coté quoted, listed

coté en Bourse quoted on the Stock Exchange, listed on the Stock Exchange

coter to quote

coter un cours acheteur to make a bid

coter un cours vendeur to make an offer

coter une échéance [*devises*] to quote a value date; [*obligations*] to quote a maturity; [*options*] to quote a month

cotisant *m* member

cotiser to contribute

coupon *m* coupon

coupon attaché cum dividend, cum div

coupon détaché ex-coupon, ex-dividend, ex-div

coupon échu ex-dividend, ex-div

coupure *f* denomination; *en petites coupures* in small denominations

courbe d'évaluation *f* pricing curve

courbe de rendement *f* yield curve

courbe de la rentabilité *f* yield curve

courbe des taux *f* yield curve, rate curve

courbe des taux d'intérêts *f* yield curve

cours *m* [*boursier*] price; *dans les cours* in the money; *hors des cours* out of the money

cours acheteur *m* bid price, offer price; *cours acheteur 22, cours vendeur 23* 22 bid, 23 offered

cours demandé *m* bid price

cours extrêmes *mpl* high and low prices

cours initial *m* initial price

cours instantané *m* current price

cours offert *m* bid price

cours officiel *m* official rate

cours spot *m* spot price

cours vendeur *m* offer price, ask price

cours à terme *m* forward price

cours au comptant *m* spot price

cours d'achat *m* bid price

cours d'action *m* share price

cours d'ouverture *m* opening price

cours de clôture *m* [*d'action*] closing price

cours de compensation *m* clearing price, settlement price

cours de règlement *m* settlement price

cours de la Bourse *m* Stock Market price

cours des changes *m* exchange rates

cours du change *m* rate of exchange

cours du jour *m* daily rate

cours du marché *m* market price, market rate; *au cours du marché* at (the) market price

court short

court terme *m* short term; *à court terme* short-term

courtage *m* brokerage

courtage officiel *m* official brokerage

courtier *m* broker

courtier-marchand de titres *m* broker-dealer

courtier en titres *m* stockbroker, broker

coût *m* cost

coût d'accès *m* [*à une sicav*] entry cost

coût de portage *m* carrying cost

coût de refinancement *m* refinancing costs

coût de transaction *m* transaction cost

coûts cachés *mpl* hidden costs

couverture *f* margin, hedge; [*activité*] hedging

couverture croisée *f* cross hedge

couverture quotidiennement actualisée *f* hedge adjusted daily

couverture de changes *f* hedging of exchange rate risks

couverture de risques *f* hedging

couverture des frais *f* cost hedging

couverture du risque de crédit *f* loan risk cover

couvrir [*frais*] to cover; [*emprunt*] to secure; [*transaction*] to hedge

se **couvrir** to hedge

se **couvrir contre** to hedge against

couvrir les engagements to cover one's exposure

couvrir un découvert to cover an overdraft

couvrir un déficit to cover a loss

couvrir un risque to hedge a risk

couvrir une position to hedge a
position
**CRB (= Comité de la
Réglementation Bancaire)** *m*
banking regulatory committee
créance *f* debt
créance commerciale *f*
commercial debt
créance douteuse *f* bad debt
créance garantie *f* secured debt
créance immobilière *f* property
debt
créance impayée *f* unpaid debt,
unrecovered debt
créance litigieuse *f* contested debt
créance non échue *f* debt not yet
due
créance principale *f* principal debt
créance privilégiée *f* preferred
debt
créance recouvrable *f* recoverable
debt
créance à recouvrer *f* outstanding
debt
créances *fpl* debts; [*comptabilité*]
receivables, accounts receivable
créances clients *fpl* accounts
receivable, trade debtors
**créances immobilisées et
douteuses** *fpl* capitalized and
bad debts
créancier *m* creditor
créancier hypothécaire *m*
mortgagee
créancier nanti *m* secured creditor
créancier obligataire *m* bond
holder
créancier ordinaire *m* ordinary
creditor, unsecured creditor
créancier privilégié *m* preferred
creditor
création monétaire *f* monetary
expansion

création de la garantie *f* creation
of the guarantee
crédit *m* credit; [*prêt*] loan; *à
crédit* credit; *acheter à crédit* to
buy on credit
crédit-acheteur *m* buyer credit
crédit auto *m* car loan
crédit back to back *m* back to
back credit
crédit-bail *m* leasing
crédit bancaire *m* bank credit; *un
crédit bancaire* a bank loan
crédit bloqué *m* frozen credit
crédit client *m* customer credit
crédit commercial commercial
credit
crédit confirmé *m* confirmed
credit
crédit consortial *m* syndicated
loan
crédit coopératif *m* cooperative
bank
crédit (à) court terme *m* short-
term credit
crédit croisé *m* cross-currency
swap
crédit cumulé *m* cumulative
credit
crédit documentaire *m*
documentary credit
crédit épargne logement *m* home
purchase loan
crédit foncier *m* land bank
crédit-fournisseur *m* supplier
credit
crédit hypothécaire *m* mortgage
loan
crédit hypothécaire à taux fixe *m*
fixed rate mortgage (loan)
crédit immobilier *m* home loan,
mortgage
crédit (à) long terme *m* long-term
credit

crédit (à) moyen terme *m* medium-term credit

crédit national *m* long-term credit bank

crédit permanent *m* revolving credit

crédit personnel *m* personal loan

crédit ponctuel *m* spot credit

crédit promoteur *m* property development loan

crédit "red clause" *m* red clause credit

crédit-relais *m* bridging loan

crédit révocable *m* callable loan

crédit revolving *m* revolving credit

crédit "sain" *m* performing loan

crédit scoring *m* credit scoring, credit rating

crédit à durée déterminée *m* fixed-term credit

crédit à durée indéterminée *m* open-ended credit

crédit à l'exportation *m* export credit

crédit à l'habitat *m* home loans; *un crédit à l'habitat* a home loan

crédit à la consommation *m* consumer credit

crédit à la consommation des ménages *m* household consumer credit

crédit à taux progressif *m* step-up rate loan

crédit à taux révisable *m* roll-over loan

crédit à taux variable *m* floating rate loan

crédit à très court terme *m* very short-term loan

crédit aux entreprises *m* business loans, corporate lending

crédit d'investissement *m* investment credit

crédit de campagne *m* stock financing loan

crédit de mobilisation de créances commerciales *m* trade receivables-backed loans

crédit de reconstitution de fonds de roulement *m* working capital facilities

crédit de sécurité *m* swing line

crédit de trésorerie *m* short-term advances, cash facilities

crédit en euro-devises *m* Euroloan

crédit par acceptation *m* acceptance credit

crédits mixtes *mpl* mixed credits

crédits de développement *mpl* development loans

créditer to credit; *créditer un compte* to credit an account; *créditer une somme sur un compte* to credit an amount to account

créditeur *m* creditor

créditeur *adj* [solde, etc.] credit; [concernant créditeurs] creditor; *être créditeur* to be in credit

crédoc *m* documentary credit

créer un chèque to write a cheque

créer une hypothèque to create a mortgage

criée: à la criée by open outcry

criminalité informatique *f* computer crime

crise boursière *f* Stock Market crisis

crise de l'endettement *f* debt crisis

croissance économique *f* economic growth

croissance monétaire f monetary growth

cross m cross trade

CT (= Court Terme) short term

cuivre m copper

cycle boursier m Stock Market cycle

D

d/a (= Documents contre Acceptation) D/A

DAB (= Distributeur Automatique de Billets) m autobank

date limite de paiement f deadline for payment

date d'échéance f due date; [de dû] maturity date; [de terme] expiry date; [de prêt] redemption date

date d'encaissement f paying-in date

date d'exigibilité f due date

date d'expiration f expiry date

date d'opération f transaction date

date de conversion f conversion date

date de jouissance f dividend entitlement date

date de levée f exercise date

date de liquidation f settlement date, liquidation date

date de paiement f payment date

date de présentation f presentation date

date de règlement f settlement date

date de remise f remittance date

date de situation f make-up date

date de validité f [de CB] validity date

date de valeur f value date

date de versement f payment date

débit m debit; *au débit de* to the debit of

débit différé m deferred debit; *carte de paiement à débit différé* deferred debit payment card

débit immédiat m immediate debit

débiter to debit; *débiter un compte* to debit an account; *débiter un compte d'une somme* to debit a sum to an account

débiteur m debtor

débiteur adj [solde] debit; *votre compte est débiteur* your account is overdrawn

débiteur concordataire m

bankrupt who has reached a
settlement with his debtors

débiteur défaillant *m* defaulter

débiteur hypothécaire *m*
mortgagor

débiteur principal *m* primary
debtor, principal debtor

débiteur solidaire *m* joint and
several debtor

déblocage du crédit *m* granting of
credit

déboires boursiers *mpl* market
setbacks

débours global *m* global outlay

déboursement *m* disbursement,
paying out

débourser to pay

décaissable [*charge*] payable

décaissement *m* cash withdrawal,
disbursement

décaisser [*montant*] to pay, to pay
out; [*TVA*] to pay

décalage *m* disparity

décalage temporel *m* timing
difference

décalage violent des marchés *m*
wide market discrepancies

décharger qn d'une dette to
discharge sb from a debt

déchéance du terme *f* event of
default

déclaration fiscale *f* tax return

déclaration de dividende *f*
declaration of a dividend,
dividend announcement

déclarer un dividende to declare a
dividend

se **déclasser** [*valeur boursière*] to
fall in value

déclinant [*marché*] declining

décloisonnement *m* deregulation

décompte *m* deduction; [*détail*]
breakdown

décompter [*déduire*] to deduct;
[*détailler*] to break down

décote *f* discount

découvert [*option*] naked

découvert *m* overdraft; *à
découvert* overdrawn; *tirer à
découvert* to overdraw one's
account; *en découvert*
overdrawn; *passer en découvert*
to go overdrawn, to go into
overdraft

découvert bancaire *m* bank
overdraft

découvert boursier *m* uncovered
position

découvert d'un compte *m*
overdraft

décrochage *m* uncoupling

décroissance *f* decrease

dédit *m* forfeit

dédommagement *m*
indemnification

déduire to deduct

défaillance *f* [*d'acheteur*] default

défaillance bancaire *f* bank
default

défaillant defaulting

défalcation *f* deduction; [*de
mauvaise créance*] writeoff

défalquer une mauvaise créance
to write off a bad debt

défalquer une somme to deduct a
sum of money

défaut de couverture *m* margin
default

défaut de paiement *m* default on
payment

défendre une devise to defend a
currency

déficit *m* deficit

déficit cumulé *m* cumulative
deficit

déficit de trésorerie *m* cash deficit

déficitaire loss-making; [*à découvert*] showing a deficit, in debit

se **dégager de ses positions** to unwind one's positions

dégager des crédits to make credit available

dégager le prix to set the price

dégager un bénéfice to show a profit, to make a profit

dégager une épargne to make a saving

dégeler des crédits to unfreeze credits

degré de solvabilité *m* credit rating

délai aller-retour *m* turnaround period

délai limite de levée *m* exercise cut-off time

délai de grâce *m* period of grace

délai de notification *m* notice date

délai de paiement *m* credit period, payment term

délai de réalisation *m* lead time

délai de règlement *m* settlement period

délai de validité *m* period of validity

délégation d'une dette *f* assignment of a debt

délégation de crédits *f* assignment of loans

délit d'initié *m* insider dealing, insider trading

délivrance d'un certificat *f* issue of a certificate

délivrance de carte bancaire *f* issue of a credit card

délivrance de titres *f* delivery of securities

délivrer des valeurs to deliver shares

délocalisation des capitaux *f* decentralization of capital

delta delta

demande *f* bid

demande d'ouverture de crédit *f* credit application, loan application

demande de monnaie *f* money demand

demande de règlement *f* request for payment

demande de renouvellement *f* re-order form

demandeur de crédit *m* loan applicant

dématérialisation *f* [*des opérations*] dematerialization, paperless handling of securities

démembré stripped

démembrement *m* stripping

démembrer [*entreprise*] to asset-strip

demi-résultat *m* half-yearly result

démonétisation *f* withdrawal from circulation, demonetization

démonétiser to demonetize, to withdraw from circulation

deniers *mpl* money, monies

dénoncer des crédits to cancel credits

dénoncer un contrat to terminate a contract

dénouer [*position*] to close out, to liquidate

dénoyautage *m* government-inspired raid on privatized company to oust shareholding supporters of the opposition party

dépassement de coût *m* cost overrun

dépasser un crédit to exceed a credit limit

dépasser un seuil to exceed a threshold

dépenser to spend

dépenses *fpl* [*débours*] expenditure, spend

dépersonnalisation *f* [*des relations*] depersonalization

déplafonner un crédit to raise the ceiling on a credit, to raise a credit limit

déport *m* discount; [*Bourse*] backwardation

déposant *m* depositor

déposer to deposit

déposer des garanties to post security

déposer un chèque to pay in a cheque

déposer une caution to lodge security, to deposit security

dépositaire *m* depositary

dépôt *m* deposit

dépôt clientèle *m* client deposits

dépôt interbancaire *m* interbank deposit

dépôt-titres *m* safe custody account; [*pour titres*] securities deposit

dépôt à terme *m* term deposit, time deposit

dépôt à vue *m* sight deposit, call deposit, demand deposit

dépôt d'épargne *m* savings deposit

dépôt d'espèces *m* cash deposit

dépôt d'une somme *m* deposit of a sum of money

dépôt de bilan *m* filing for bankruptcy

dépôt de garantie *m* initial margin, margin

dépôts à court terme *mpl* short-term deposits

dépôts d'espèces *mpl* cash deposits

dépréciation *f* depreciation; [*de créances*] write-down

dépréciation d'actif *f* asset depreciation

se **déprécier** to depreciate

déprécier la valeur de to lower the value of

déréglementation bancaire *f* deregulation of the banking system

déréglementation financière *f* financial deregulation

déréglementer to deregulate

dérivé: produit dérivé *m* derivative

dérivé d'actions *m* equity(-based) derivative

dérivé d'assurance *m* insurance derivative

dérivé d'une monnaie *m* currency derivative

dérivé de crédit *m* credit derivative

dernier jour de transaction *m* last trading day

désapprovisionné [*compte*] overdrawn

désendettement *m* reduction in borrowings, reduction in gearing

déshypothéquer to lift a mortgage from

désinflation *f* disinflation

désintéresser un créancier to pay off a creditor

désintermédiation *f* disintermediation, removal of the middle man

désintermédier to disintermediate

désinvestir des capitaux to divest

désinvestissement *m* divestment

desk d'options *m* options desk

déstabilisateur destabilizing

déstabiliser to destabilize

détachement à la cote *m* delisting

détacher à la cote to delist

détaxation (de) *f* removal of tax (on)

détenir 5% du capital de to hold 5% of the shares in, to have a 5% shareholding in

détenir des actions to hold shares

détenir en garantie to hold as security

détenteur *m* holder

détenteur direct d'actions *m* direct shareholder

détenteur d'obligations *m* bondholder

détenteur d'un compte *m* account holder

détenteur d'une option *m* holder of an option, option holder

détenteur de titres *m* shareholder

détention *f* holding

détermination des prix *f* price setting, price fixing

détourner de l'argent to embezzle money

dette *f* debt

dette antérieure *f* prior debt

dette consolidée *f* consolidated debt

dette financière *f* financial debt

dette foncière *f* property charge; [*hypothécaire*] mortgage debt

dette privilégiée *f* preferred debt

dette véreuse *f* bad debt

dettes représentées par un titre *fpl* debts evidenced by a certificate

dettes subordonnées *fpl* subordinated debts

dettes à court terme *fpl* current liabilities

dévalorisation *f* loss of value

dévaluer to devalue

devis *m* estimate

devise *f* currency

devise étrangère *f* foreign currency

devise-titre *f* foreign security exchange currency

devises étrangères *fpl* foreign currency

devoir to owe

devoir fiduciaire *m* fiduciary duty

devoir de vigilance *m* duty of vigilance

diagnostic *m* analysis

diagnostic financier *m* financial health check

différence de cours *f* rate difference, difference in the rate

différences positives/négatives de change *fpl* foreign exchange gains/losses

différentiel de taux *m* rate differential

différentiel de taux d'intérêt *m* interest rate differential

différer le paiement to defer payment

difficultés de trésorerie *fpl* cashflow difficulties

diffusion de cours *f* price dissemination

diminution du capital *f* reduction of capital

directeur *m* [*d'une succursale*] manager

directeur d'agence *m* branch manager

directeur de banque *m* bank manager

directeur de marché *m* [*de la place de Paris*] market director

directeur de succursale *m* branch manager

directeur de l'informatique *m* EDP manager

directeur de la clientèle *m* customer relations manager

direction clientèle entreprises *f* corporate lending department

direction financière *f* financial management; [*service*] finance department

direction des crédits *f* credit management; [*service*] credit department

dirigeant d'OPCVM *m* fund manager

disponibilités *fpl* liquid assets

disponibilités en caisse et en banque *fpl* cash on hand and at bank

disponible available; [*actif*] liquid

disposer un chèque sur to draw a cheque on

disposer d'une somme to have a sum of money at one's disposal

dissolution d'une société *f* winding up of a company

dissoudre to wind up

dissymétrie des risques *f* risk asymmetry

distribuer un dividende to pay a dividend

distributeur automatique *m* dispensing machine, cash dispenser

distributeur automatique de billets *m* automatic cash dispenser, autobank, automatic teller machine *Am*

distributeur d'espèces *m* cash dispenser

distributeur de billets *m* cash machine, cashpoint machine

distribution d'un bénéfice *f* distribution of profit

distribution de dividende *f* payment of a dividend

distribution de prêts *f* granting of loans

diversification des placements *f* spread of investments

diversification des risques *f* risk diversification

dividende *m* dividend

dividende brut *m* gross dividend

dividende cumulatif *m* cumulative dividend

dividende définitif *m* final dividend

dividende final *m* final dividend

dividende intérimaire *m* interim dividend

dividende intermédiaire *m* interim dividend

dividende net *m* net dividend

dividende supplémentaire *m* extra dividend

dividende d'action *m* share dividend, scrip dividend

dividendes accrus *mpl* accrued dividends

division financière *f* financial division

division d'actions *f* share split

documents contre acceptation documents against acceptance

documents contre paiement documents against payment

doit et avoir *m* debits and credits

dollar américain *m* American dollar, US dollar

domaine financier *m* financial field

domicile *m* domicile

domiciliataire *m* [*d'effet*] paying agent; [*de chèque*] paying bank

domiciliation *f* domiciliation
domiciliation bancaire *f* paying bank
domicilier to domicile
données financières *fpl* financial data
donneur d'aval *m* guarantor
donneur d'ordre *m* principal, order-giver
donneur d'option *m* taker for a put and call
dossier *m* file
dossier de crédit *m* credit file
dossier de (demande de) crédit *m* loan application
dotation *f* allocation
doté allocated
double tarification *f* double charging
doublé: option d'achat doublé à la baisse put of twice more; **option d'achat doublée à la hausse** call of twice more
d/p (= Documents contre Paiement) D/P
drainer des fonds to tap funds
droit bancaire *m* banking law
droit détaché ex-rights
droit au bail *m* [*bien incorporel*] leasehold
droit d'attribution *m* right of assignment
droit d'option *m* option right
droit de courtage *m* brokerage (fee)
droit de gage *m* right of lien
droit de rachat *m* repurchase right, buyback right

droit de rétention *m* lien
droit de souscription *m* warrant
droit de tirage spécial *m* special drawing right
droit des cartes de paiement et de crédit *m* debit and credit card law
droits d'entrée *mpl* [*souscription de titres*] front-end fees
droits attachés cum rights
droits de garde *mpl* safe custody fees
droits de sortie *mpl* [*souscription de titres*] back-end fees
droits de timbre *mpl* stamp duty
droits de tirage *mpl* drawing rights
droits de tirage spéciaux *mpl* special drawing rights
droits préférentiels de souscription *mpl* pre-emptive rights
DTS (= Droits de Tirage Spéciaux) *mpl* SDR
dû due, owing; *en due forme* in due form
durée résiduelle *f* remaining duration
durée de crédit *f* term of loan
durée de validité *f* period of validity
durée de validité d'un ordre *f* duration of validity of an order
durée de vie *f* [*d'une option*] lifetime
dynamisme *m* [*du marché*] buoyancy

E

EBE (= Excédent Brut d'Exploitation) *m* EBDIT, PBDIT

écart *m* spread

écart diagonal *m* diagonal spread

écart horizontal *m* horizontal spread

écart net *m* net variance

écart type *m* standard deviation

écart vertical *m* vertical spread

écart de prime *m* option spread

écart des cours *m* price spread

écarts de conversion *mpl* exchange adjustments

écarts de réévaluation *mpl* revaluation reserve

échange cambiste *m* treasury swap

échange financier *m* swap

échange interbancaire *m* interbank trading

échange de créances *m* debt swap

échange de créances contre actifs *m* debt equity swap

échange de devises *m* currency swap

échange de données informatisé *m* electronic data interchange

échange de marchandises *m* exchange of goods

échange de taux d'intérêt *m* interest rate swap

échange de taux sur devises *m* combined interest rate and currency swap, CIRCUS

échanges commerciaux *mpl* commercial transactions

échappatoire fiscal *m* tax loophole

échéance *f* [*de lettre de change*] maturity; [*de bail*] expiry date; **arriver à échéance le ...** to become due on ...; **avant l'échéance** before expiry

échéance contractuelle *f* fixed maturity date

échéance éloignée *f* long maturity, far month

échéance emprunt *f* loan maturity

échéance proche *f* short maturity, near month

échéance à vue *f* sight maturity

échéances de fin de mois *fpl* end of month payments

échéancier *m* due date file, aged debtor schedule

échelle mobile *f* sliding scale; [*clause*] escalator clause

échelle d'intérêts *f* scale of interest

échelon de cotation *m* tick size, tick

échelonner des paiements to stagger payments, to spread out payments

échoir to fall due

économétrique econometric

économie bancaire *f* banking economics

économie monétaire *f* monetary economics

économie des marchés *f* market economy

économies *fpl* savings

écoulement *m* turnover

écrasement des marges *m* squeeze on margins

écritures *fpl* accounts

écritures comptables *fpl* book-keeping entries

écu *m* ECU

Écureuil *m* collective body in charge of bond issues for savings and providential institutions

EDI (= Échange de Données Informatisé) *m* EDI

édition d'un contrat d'assurance *f* issuing of an insurance policy

effectuer un paiement to make a payment

effectuer des règlements to make payments

effet *m* bill, draft; [*titre*] security

effet balançoire *m* see-saw effect

effet endossé *m* endorsed bill

effet escompté *m* discounted bill

effet réducteur *m* downward effect

effet saisonnier *m* seasonal effect

effet à courte échéance *m* short-dated bill, short

effet à date fixe *m* fixed-date bill

effet à longue échéance *m* long-dated bill, long

effet à ordre *m* promissory note

effet à rendement variable *m* variable-yield security

effet à taux flottant *m* floating-rate note, FRN

effet à taux révisable *m* floating rate note, FRN

effet à vue *m* sight bill

effet à l'encaissement *m* bill for collection

effet au porteur *m* bearer bill, bill made out to bearer

effet de change *m* bill of exchange

effet de commerce *m* bill, commercial bill

effet de levier *m* leverage; *à fort effet de levier* highly leveraged

effet en blanc *m* blank draft

effet en souffrance *m* dishonoured bill

effet sans protêt *m* bill "without protest"

effet sur place *m* local bill, town bill

effets de commerce en eurodevises *mpl* Eurocommercial paper

effort d'épargne *m* savings initiative

effritement des cours *m* erosion of prices

émetteur *m* issuer

émetteur (d'options) couvert *m* covered writer (of options)

émetteur d'une option *m* writer of an option

émetteur de cartes *m* card issuer

émettre un emprunt to issue loan stock, to make a bond issue

émettre un chèque to issue a cheque, to write out a cheque

émettre des actions to issue shares

émission *f* issue, issuance

émission boursière *f* share issue

émission obligataire *f* bond issue

émission d'actions *f* share issue

émission d'actions gratuites *f* bonus issue, scrip issue

émission d'actions en bourse *f* flotation

émission d'emprunts *f* issuing of loans

émission d'obligations *f* bond issue

émission de droits de participation *f* rights issue

émission de droits de souscription *f* rights issue

émission de moyens de paiement *f* issuing of payment instruments

employé de banque *m* bank employee, bank clerk

emprunt *m* loan

emprunt garanti *m* secured loan

emprunt indexé *m* indexed loan

emprunt obligataire *m* bond issue, loan stock; [*titre*] debenture bond

emprunt obligataire convertible *m* convertible loan stock

emprunt participatif *m* equity loan issue

emprunt à court terme *m* short-term loan

emprunt à long terme *m* long-term loan

emprunt d'État *m* government bond

emprunt d'État à dix ans *m* 10-year government bond

emprunt d'État de référence *m* benchmark government bond

emprunts à court terme *mpl* short-term borrowings

emprunts à long terme *mpl* long-term borrowings

emprunts et dettes financières *mpl* bank and other financial borrowings

emprunter to borrow

emprunter de l'argent à to borrow money from

emprunter sur to borrow against

emprunteur *m* borrower

emprunteur *adj* borrowing

emprunteur non bancaire *m* non-bank borrower

encadrement du crédit *m* credit restriction, credit squeeze, credit control

encaissable cashable

encaisse *f* cash in till

encaisse(s) *f(pl)* cash

encaisse métallique *f* cash and bullion

encaissement *m* collection; [*de chèque*] paying in, encashment *Br*

encaisser to collect; [*chèque*] to cash, to encash *Br*; [*sur son compte*] to pay in

encaisser de l'argent to receive money; [*sur son compte*] to pay in cash

encaisser un premium to receive a premium

encourir des frais to incur costs

encours *m* loans outstanding, exposure

encours débiteur autorisé *m* authorized overdraft facility

encours douteux *mpl* non-performing loans, bad debts

encours de crédit *m* loan book, loans outstanding

encours des créances *m* loans outstanding

endetté in debt

endetté en dollars having dollar debts

endettement *m* indebtedness, gearing

endettement à long terme *m* long-term indebtedness

endettement à moyen terme *m* medium-term indebtedness

endettement à terme *m* long-term debt

*s'***endetter** to get into debt
endos *m* endorsement
endossable endorsable
endossataire *mf* endorsee
endossement *m* endorsement
endosser to endorse
endosser en blanc to blank endorse
endosseur *m* endorser
engagement *m* commitment; *sans engagement* without commitment
engagement immobilier *m* property commitment
engagement de payer *m* obligation to pay
engagements à la Bourse *mpl* Stock Exchange commitments
engager des capitaux to invest capital
enregistrement comptable sincère *m* honest accounting
enregistrement horodaté *m* date-stamped record
enregistrer une garantie to register a guarantee
enregistrer une perte to show a loss, to record a loss
enseigne bancaire *f* big bank
*s'***entendre sur un prix** to agree on a price
entraîner une perte to incur a loss
entreprise cible *f* target company
entrer en position courte to take a short position
environnement bancaire *m* banking environment
épargnant *m* saver
épargne *f* savings; [*activité*] saving
épargne nouvelle *f* new savings
épargne retraite *f* retirement savings
épargne salariale *f* save as you earn

épargne des menages *f* household saving
épargner to save
éponger des dettes to absorb debts
équilibre monétaire *m* monetary equilibrium
équilibre des marchés *m* market equilibrium
équilibrer to balance
*s'***équilibrer** to even out
érosion *f* [*des bons de caisse*] erosion
errement du marché *m* market fluctuation
escomptable discountable
escompte *m* discount
escompte commercial *m* trade discounting
escompte officiel *m* bank discount rate
escompter to discount
escompter une hausse to anticipate an increase
escroquerie *f* fraud
espèces *fpl* cash
espèces en caisse *fpl* cash on hand
établir un chèque to make out a cheque, to write a cheque
établir un chèque à l'ordre de to make a cheque payable to
établissement bancaire *m* bank
établissement collecteur de dépôts *m* deposit-taking institution
établissement dépositaire de titres *m* share custody institution
établissement financier *m* financial institution
établissement payeur *m* paying bank
établissement teneur du compte *m* account-holding organization
établissement d'un compte *m*

opening an account, setting up an account

établissement de crédit *m* credit institution

établissement des cours *m* price fixing

étain *m* tin

étalement *m* spreading, staggering

étaler sur plusieurs exercices to spread (out) over several financial years

étalon monétaire *m* monetary standard

étalon or *m* gold standard

état *m* [*relevé*] statement

état financier *m* financial statement

état imprimé *m* printed statement

état d'un compte *m* position on an account

état de compte *m* statement of account

état de fortune *m* personal wealth statement, personal financial statement

état du marché *m* state of the market

ETE (= Excédent de Trésorerie d'Exploitation) *m* cashflow from operations

éteindre une dette to pay off a debt

étendue *f* [*de variables*] range

étendue d'une perte *f* extent of a loss

étude du risque *f* risk analysis

eurobanque *f* Eurobank

eurochèque *m* Eurocheque

eurocrédit *m* Euroloan

eurodevise *f* Eurocurrency

eurodollar *m* Eurodollar

euro-émission *f* Euro-issue

euro-emprunt *m* Euroloan

eurofranc *m* Eurofranc

euro-obligation *f* Eurobond

évaluation par score *f* credit scoring

évaluer to value

évasion de capitaux *f* flight of capital

excédent brut d'exploitation *m* gross operating profit

excédent net d'exploitation *m* net operating profit

excédent de dépôt de garantie *m* excess margin

excédent de trésorerie d'exploitation *m* cashflow from operations

excès de trésorerie *m* cash surplus

exécuter en temps réel to process in real time

exécution [*d'un ordre*] *f* execution

exécution au prix du marché *f* execution at market

exempt d'impôts tax-free

exerçable exercisable

exercer [*une option*] to exercise

exercer à l'échéance to exercise at maturity

exercer par anticipation to exercise in advance

exercice *m* financial year, fiscal year *Am*; [*d'une option*] exercise

exercice automatique *m* automatic exercise

exercice prématuré *m* early exercise, premature exercise

exigibilité: date d'exigibilité *f* due date

exigibilité immédiate immediately due

exigible payable, due

exonération *f* exemption

expert-comptable *m* chartered accountant *Br*, certified public accountant *Am*

expert financier *m* financial expert

expiration *f* expiry

expirer to expire

exploitant de banque *m* banking operative

exploitation bancaire *f* banking sector

exportation *f* export

s'**exposer aux risques** to take on risks; *s'exposer davantage aux risques* to increase its/their risk exposure

exposition aux risques *f* exposure, risk exposure

expropriation *f* expropriation

exproprier to expropriate

extinction d'une dette *f* discharge of a debt

extra-comptable [*ajustement*] off-balance sheet

extrait de compte *m* statement of account; [*banque*] bank statement, statement of account

face à face *m* private inter-company loan without bank involvement

facilité d'émission de billets *f* note issuance facility, NIF

facilité de caisse *f* cash facility

facteur technique *m* technical factor

facteur temps *m* time factor

facturation *f* invoicing, billing

facture *f* invoice

facture électronique *f* electronic invoice

facture d'avoir *f* credit note

facture de débit *f* debit note

facture de doit *f* debit note

facturette *f* imprinter

faibles variations de cours *fpl* small price movements, slight price movements

faiblir [*cours*] to weaken

failli *m* bankrupt

failli concordataire *m* bankrupt who has reached a settlement with his debtors

failli non réhabilité *m* undischarged bankrupt

failli réhabilité *m* discharged bankrupt

faillite *f* bankruptcy; *faire faillite* to go bankrupt; *être en faillite* to be bankrupt

faire un prix to quote a price

faire un versement to pay in, to

pay money in
falsification *f* forgery
faute professionnelle *f* professional misconduct
faute de paiement for non-payment
faute de provision for lack of funds
faux chèque *m* forged cheque
faveur: en faveur de in favour of
Fbe (= Fédération Bancaire Européenne) *f* EBF
FCP (= Fonds Commun de Placement) *m* investment trust, mutual fund
FCPE (= Fonds Commun de Placement d'Entreprise) *m* company investment fund
FDM (= Fin De Mois) end of month
Fed *f* [*aux USA*] Fed, Federal Reserve System
FER (= Fonds d'Épargne pour la Retraite, Fonds d'Épargne-Retraite) *m* retirement savings fund
fer-blanc *m* tin
ferme firm; *acheter ferme* to make a firm purchase
fermer to close
fermer un compte to close an account
fermer une position to close (out) a position
fermeté des cours *f* firmness of prices, steadiness of prices
fermeté du marché *f* steadiness of the market
fermeture *f* closing
fermeture d'un compte *f* closing of an account
fermeture de position *f* closure of a position

feuille de versement *f* paying-in slip, pay-in slip
feuillet *m* sheet
fiche d'imputation *f* data entry form
fiche d'imputation comptable *f* accounts record form
fichier central des incidents de paiement *m* central register of unpaid trade bills
fichier client *m* client file
fidéicommis *m* trust; *tenir qch par fidéicommis* to hold sth in trust
fiduciaire *mf* trustee
fiduciaire *adj* fiduciary; *monnaie fiduciaire* paper money
filiale de banque *f* bank branch
filialiser to decentralize
filière électronique *f* electronic transfer
finance *f* finance
financement *m* financing
financement bancaire *m* bank finance, bank financing, bank funding
financement direct *m* direct financing
financement extérieur *m* external financing
financement immobilier *m* property finance
financement à court terme *m* short-term financing
financement à long terme *m* long-term financing
financement à moyen terme *m* medium-term financing
financement des exportations *m* export finance, export financing
financement par endettement *m* debt financing
financement sur endettement *m* debt financing

financement sur fonds propres *m*
own-funds financing
financer to finance, to fund
financiarisation *f* increasingly
financial nature
financier *m* financier
financier *adj* financial
financièrement financially
fin: de fin de mois end-of-month
fin de l'exercice *f* end of the
financial year; *de fin d'exercice*
year-end; *en fin d'exercice* at
the end of the financial year
fine: in fine bullet
fisc *m* tax authorities, tax man
fiscal fiscal
fiscaliste *mf* tax specialist
fiscalité *f: fiscalité excessive*
excessive taxation; *optimiser la
fiscalité de* to improve the tax-
efficiency of
fixation des prix *f* price fixing
fixe [*taux de change*] fixed; *à taux
fixe* fixed-rate
fixer un prix to fix a price
fléchir to ease
fléchissement des prix *m* fall in
prices
flexible flexible
float *m* float
flottant *m* float
flottant bancaire *m* bank float
flotter to float; *faire flotter* to
float
fluctuation des cours *f* exchange
rate fluctuation; price fluctuation
fluctuations de taux d'intérêt *fpl*
interest rate fluctuations
fluctuer to fluctuate
**FLUX (= Franc
LUXembourgeois)** *m*
Luxembourg franc
flux financier *m* flow of finance

flux financier anticipé *m*
expected financial flow
flux monétaire *m* cashflow
flux moyen *m* [*de mouvements sur
les comptes*] average movement
flux d'annuités *m* annuity flow
flux de trésorerie *m* cashflow
flux des fonds *m* flow of funds
**FMI (= Fonds Monétaire
International)** *m* IMF
foncière *f* property
fonds commun de placement *m*
investment trust, mutual fund
**fonds commun de placement
d'entreprise** *m* company
investment fund, corporate
investment fund
fonds fédéraux américains *mpl*
(American) Federal Funds, Fed
Funds
Fonds monétaire international *m*
International Monetary Fund
fonds propres *mpl* equity, own
funds
fonds publics *mpl* Government
funds; [*valeurs*] Government
stocks
fonds d'épargne-retraite *m*
retirement savings fund
fonds d'épargne pour la retraite
m retirement savings fund
fonds d'État *mpl* Government
funds
fonds d'investissement *m*
investment fund
fonds de garantie *m* reserve fund
fonds de garantie professionnel
m deposit protection scheme
fonds de pension *m* pension fund
**fonds de pension par
capitalisation** *m* funded pension
scheme
fonds de retraite *m* pension fund

fonds de roulement *m* working capital

fonds pour risques bancaires généraux *m* general provisions

fongible fungible

forclusion *f* foreclosure

forfait *m* lump sum; **à forfait** à forfait, non-recourse

forfaitage *m* forfaiting

forfaitaire in one amount, lump-sum

forfaitairement in a lump sum

forfaitisation *f* forfaiting

formation du cours *f* price formation

formule de calcul *f* mathematical formula

formule de chèque *f* cheque form

formule de crédit *f* credit application form

forte hausse *f* sharp rise

forte somme *f* large sum of money

fourchette de prix *f* price range

fournir des fonds to provide funds

foyer fiscal *m* tax domicile

fraction *f* fraction

fraction d'intérêt *f* interest accrued

fractionnement *m* [*d'actions*] share split

fractionner des actions to split shares

fragilisation d'une monnaie *f* weakening of a currency

frais bancaires *mpl* bank charges

frais encourus *mpl* costs incurred

frais financiers *mpl* financial costs

frais financiers nets *mpl* net financial costs

frais généraux *mpl* overheads *Br*, overhead *Am*

frais d'administration *mpl* administrative costs; [*en échange d'un service*] handling charge

frais d'entrée *mpl* [*d'une sicav*] front-end fees, front-load fees

frais de banque *mpl* bank charges

frais de commission *mpl* commission costs

frais de compensation *mpl* clearing fees

frais de dossier *mpl* administration fee

frais de négociation *mpl* trading fees

frais de sortie *mpl* [*d'une sicav*] back-end fees, back-load fees

frais de tenue de compte *mpl* account management charge, account management fee

frais de transaction *mpl* transaction costs

franc *m* franc

franc or *m* gold value of the franc

franchir la barre (de 107) to break through the (107) barrier

fraude *f* fraud

fraudeur *m* defrauder, swindler

frauduleusement fraudulently

frauduleux fraudulent

front-office *m* front office

fructifier: faire fructifier qch to make sth yield a profit

fructueux profitable

fuite de capitaux *f* flight of capital

fusion *f* merger

fusionner to merge

G

GAB (= Guichet Automatique de Banque) *m* automatic cash dispenser, ATM
gagé pledged
gage immobilier *m* charge over property
gager qch to deposit sth as security, to pledge sth as security
gageur *m* pledgor
gagiste *mf* pledgee
gagnant profitable
gagner gros to make large profits
gagner de l'argent to earn money
gain *m* profit
gain illimité *m* unlimited profit
gain limité *m* limited profit
gain potentiel *m* potential profit
gain d'argent *m* financial gain
gain de change *m* exchange rate gain, exchange gain
gain de portage *m* carrying gain
gamma *m* gamma
gamme de prix *f* price range
gamme de stratégies *f* range of strategies
gap *m* [*de taux fixe*] gap
garant *m* guarantor; [*d'émission d'actions*] underwriter
garant solidaire *m* joint and several guarantor
garantie *f* guarantee
garantie bancaire *f* bank guarantee

garantie à première demande *f* first demand guarantee
garantie d'émission *f* underwriting
garantie de reprise *f* [*d'obligation*] repurchase agreement
garantie de solvabilité *f* liquidity guarantee
garantie du capital *f* capital guarantee
garantie sur le rendement *f* guaranteed yield
garantir to guarantee, to collateralize; [*émission d'actions*] to underwrite
garantir la solvabilité de qn to guarantee sb's creditworthiness
garantir un emprunt to secure a loan; [*obligataire*] to underwrite a bond issue
garde *f* custody
garde en dépôt *f* safe custody
Gebc (= Groupement Européen des Banques Coopératives) *m* European cooperative banks group
Gece (= Groupement Européen des Caisses d'Épargne) *m* European savings banks group
gel de crédits *m* credit freeze
gelé [*crédits*] frozen
Gema (= Groupement des Entreprises Mutuelles

d'Assurance) *m* group of
mutual insurance companies

gérant de portefeuille *m* fund
manager

gérer des actifs to manage assets

gérer un compte to manage an
account

gestion active de portefeuille *f*
active portfolio management

gestion clientèle *f* client
management

gestion électronique de factures *f*
electronic invoice management

gestion financière *f* financial
management

gestion multidevises *f*
multicurrency management

gestion patrimoniale *f* asset
management

gestion d'actifs *f* asset
management

gestion d'alertes *f* early warning
system

gestion de biens *f* asset
management

gestion de capitaux *f* fund
management

gestion de crédit *f* credit
management

gestion de fonds *f* fund
management

gestion de patrimoine *f* asset
management

gestion de la trésorerie *f* cashflow
management

gestion de portefeuille *f* portfolio
management, fund management

gestion des impayés *f* debt
management

gestion des incidents de paiement
f payments management

gestion des liquidités *f* cash
management

gestion des risques *f* risk
management

gestion du portefeuille de prêts *f*
loan portfolio management

gestion du risque client *f* client
risk management

gestionnaire de fortune *m*
manager of an important
account

gestionnaire de patrimoine *m*
asset manager

global: somme globale *f* lump
sum

globalement globally

globalisation *f* globalization

se **globaliser** to become globalized

gonflement du volume du crédit
m increase in bank lending

**Gouverneur de la Banque de
France** *m* Governor of the Bank
of France

**GPTR (= Groupement des
Porteurs de Titres Russes)** *m*
Association of Russian
bondholders

grand investisseur *m* big investor

grande banque *f* big bank, major
bank

greenmail *m* greenmail

grevé [*bien*] encumbered

grevé de dettes saddled with debts

grever to encumber

grille de score *f* scoring grid

gros dépôt *m* wholesale deposit

groupe bancaire *m* banking group

**Groupement des porteurs de
titres russes** *m* Association of
Russian bondholders

guichet *m* counter, window, wicket
Am; [*succursale*] branch

guichet automatique *m* autobank

guichet automatique de banque
m automatic cash dispenser

guichet permanent *m* autobank
guichet de banque *m* position, bank counter

guichetier *m* bank clerk, bank teller, teller

habilité [*établissement*] authorized
habilité à signer authorized to sign
hausse: en hausse de up by
hausse inopinée (des cours) *f* unexpected rise in prices
hausse limitée (des cours) *f* slight firming (of prices)
hausse de faible amplitude *f* slight rise
hausse des cours *f* Stock Market rise
hausse sur un an *f* year-on-year increase
haussier [*marché boursier*] bull, bullish
haut de bilan *m* top half of the balance sheet
hauteur: à hauteur de to the tune of
heure d'ouverture *f* opening time
heure de fermeture *f* closing time
heures d'ouverture *fpl* opening hours; [*de la Bourse*] trading hours; [*d'une banque*] banking

hours
honorer ses échéances to pay on the due date
horaires criés *mpl* trading hours
horizon d'anticipation *m* horizon of expectation
hors bilan off-balance sheet; *opérations de hors bilan* off-balance sheet transactions
hors comptabilité off-balance sheet
hors cote: marché hors cote unlisted market, over-the-counter market
hybride hybrid
hypothécable mortgageable
hypothécaire mortgage
hypothèque *f* mortgage
hypothèque de premier rang *f* first legal mortgage
hypothéquer un bien to mortgage an asset
hypothèses de volatilité *fpl* volatility assumptions

I

IEIF (= Institut de l'Épargne Immobilière et Foncière) *m* property savings institute

IFNB (= Institution Financière Non Bancaire) *f* non-bank financial institution

illiquide illiquid; *actif illiquide* non-liquid asset

image-chèque *f* picture cheque

immobilier *m* property

immobilier d'entreprise *m* commercial property

immobilisation *f* fixed asset

immobilisation corporelle *f* tangible fixed asset

immobilisation financière *f* long-term investment

immobilisation incorporelle *f* intangible fixed asset

immobilisation d'une couverture *f* locking in a hedge

immobilisation de capitaux *f* tied up capital, capital assets

immobiliser [*des fonds*] to tie up

immobiliser une couverture to lock in a hedge

impayé *m* outstanding debt; [*facture*] unpaid bill; *tomber en impayé* to default

impayé *adj* outstanding

importance d'un crédit *f* size of a loan

importation *f* import

impôt *m* tax

impôt de Bourse *m* transaction tax, Stock Exchange tax

imprimé *m* [*formulaire*] form

imputable chargeable

imputation (à) *f* charge (to)

imputer qch sur to charge sth to

inactif [*marché*] slack

inanimé [*marché*] sluggish

incessibilité *f* non-transferability

incessible non-transferable

incidence: avoir une incidence sur le cours to have an impact on price

incidences fiscales *fpl* tax impact

inconvertible non-convertible

incotable untrad(e)able

incoté [*cours*] unquoted

indemnisable compensable

indemnisation *f* compensation

indemniser to compensate; *indemniser qn de qch* to compensate sb for sth

indemnité *f* compensation

indemnité de retard *f* late payment penalty

indexation *f* indexation, index-linking

indexé index-linked

indicateur économique *m* economic indicator

indice actions *m* share index

indice boursier *m* share index, stock index, Stock Market index

indice CAC 40 *m* CAC 40 index, *French equivalent to FTSE*

indice clé *m* key index

indice composite *m* composite index

indice DAX 30 *m* DAX 30 index

indice Dow Jones *m* Dow Jones index

indice FT 100 *m* FT 100 index

indice Nikkei *m* Nikkei index

indice S&P *m* Standard and Poors index

indice de compensation *m* daily closing price

indice de liquidation *m* settlement price

indice des cours d'actions *m* share price index

indice des prix de détail *m* retail price index

indiquer un prix to quote a price

indivision *f* joint possession

industrie bancaire mondiale *f* world banking industry

inéchangeable non-exchangeable

inescomptable undiscountable

inexécution d'un contrat *f* non-performance of a contract

inexigible not due

in fine bullet

inflation des prix *f* price inflation

inflation par la demande *f* demand-pull inflation

inflation par les coûts *f* cost-push inflation

informatique *f* electronic data processing

informatique bancaire *f* computerized banking

informatisation *f* computerization

informatisé computerized

informatiser to computerize

ingénierie financière *f* corporate finance

injonction à l'achat *f* buy order

injonction à la vente *f* sell order

inscription hypothécaire *f* registration of a mortgage

inscriptions nominatives *fpl* registered shares

inscrire à la cote to list

s'inscrire en baisse [*actions, cours*] to fall

s'inscrire en hausse [*actions, cours*] to rise; **s'inscrire en hausse de 18%** to rise by 18%

insolvabilité *f* insolvency

insolvable insolvent

inspecteur chargé des réclamations *m* complaints manager

instabilité des cours *f* unsteadiness of prices, price instability

instable [*marché boursier*] unsettled

Institut monétaire européen *m* European Monetary Institute

institut d'émission *m* issuing house

institut de crédit *m* credit institution

institution financière *f* financial institution

institution de crédit *f* credit institution

institutions article 99 *fpl* securities houses

institutionnel *m* institutional investor

instruction d'exercice *f* exercise instruction

instrument financier *m* financial instrument

instrument financier à terme *m* financial future

instrument de crédit *m* credit instrument

instrument de maîtrise du risque *m* risk management tool

instrument de marché *m* market instrument

instrument de paiement *m* payment instrument

insuffisance de provision *f* insufficient funds

insuffisance de trésorerie *f* cash shortage

intégralement libéré fully paid up

intégration financière *f* financial integration

interbancaire interbank

interbancarité *f* interoperability

interconnexion *f* interconnection

interentreprise intercompany

intéressement *m* [*aux résultats*] profit-sharing, profit-sharing scheme

intérêt *m* interest; *qui produit intérêt* interest-bearing; *porter/ rapporter des intérêts* to bear/ yield interest

intérêt annuel *m* annual interest

intérêt bancaire *m* bank interest

intérêt composé *m* compound interest

intérêt couru *m* accrued interest

intérêt fixe *m* fixed interest

intérêt servi *m* interest paid

intérêt simple *m* simple interest

intérêt variable *m* variable-rate interest

intérêt de retard *m* interest on late payment, interest on arrears

intérêt du marché *m* open interest

intérêts accumulés *mpl* accrued interest

intérêts arriérés *mpl* back interest

intérêts bruts *mpl* gross interest

intérêts composés *mpl* compound interest

intérêts créditeurs *mpl* credit interest

intérêts débiteurs *mpl* debit interest

intérêts dus *mpl* interest due

intérêts échus *mpl* accrued interest, outstanding interest

intérêts échus et non payés *mpl* overdue interest

intérêts exigibles *mpl* interest due (and payable)

intérêts intérimaires *mpl* broken interest

intérêts moratoires *mpl* default interest, penalty interest

intérêts perçus *mpl* interest received

intérêts versés *mpl* interest paid

intérêts à échoir *mpl* accruing interest

intermédiaire bancaire *m* banking intermediary

intermédiaire compensateur *m* clearing member

intermédiaire financier *m* financial intermediary

intermédiaire négociateur *m* trading member

intermédiation *f* intermediation

intermédié [*système*] intermediated

interopérabilité *f* interoperability

interopérable interoperable

interrompre un crédit to foreclose on a loan

intervenant *m* market player

intransférabilité *f* non-transferability

intransférable non-transferable

intransmissibilité *f* [*d'un capital*] non-transferability

intransmissible non-transferable

introduction en Bourse *f* listing on the Stock Exchange

introduire en Bourse [*une valeur*] to list on the Stock Exchange, to quote on the Stock Exchange

investir to invest

investir à court terme to make a short-term investment, to invest short-term

investir à long terme to make a long-term investment, to invest long-term

investir à moyen terme to make a medium-term investment

investissement *m* investment

investissement à court terme *m* short-term investment

investissement à long terme *m* long-term investment

investissement à l'étranger *m* overseas investment, foreign investment

investissement de capitaux *m* capital investment

investissements productifs *mpl* interest-bearing investments

investisseur *m* investor

investisseur étranger *m* overseas investor, foreign investor

investisseur institutionnel *m* institutional investor

investisseur privé *m* private investor

irrachetable [*obligation*] irredeemable

irrégulier [*marché boursier*] unsteady

irremboursable [*obligation*] irredeemable

irrévocabilité *f* irrevocability

irrévocable irrevocable

irriguer le marché to release funds into the market

J

jeu à la hausse *m* bull trade

jeu de bourse *m* Stock Market gamble

jeu du marché *m* vagaries of the market

J.J. (= au Jour le Jour) overnight

jouer: faire jouer une garantie to invoke a guarantee, to call a guarantee

jouer qch to play sth

jouer à la baisse to take a bear position

jouer à la hausse to take a bull position
jouer en Bourse to speculate, to play the market
jouissance d'intérêts *f* entitlement to interest
jour chômé *m* public holiday
jour férié *m* public holiday
jour franc *m* clear day
jour ouvrable *m* business day, working day
jour ouvré *m* working day
jours d'intérêt *mpl* interest days
jour de Bourse *m* trading day
jour de grâce *m* day of grace
jour de liquidation *m* account day, settlement day
jour de paiement *m* payment day
jour de valeur *m* value date
journal financier *m* financial newspaper
journal de banque *m* bank book
journal de la Bourse *m* Stock Exchange journal
journée comptable *f* accounting day
journée de Bourse *f* trading day
jugement déclaratif de faillite *m* adjudication in bankruptcy
juriste de banque *m* banking lawyer

keynésien Keynesian
KF (= KiloFranc) K
kilofranc *m* thousand francs

krach boursier *m* Stock Exchange crash, Stock Market crash

L

laminage de marges *m* squeezing of margins

lancer des titres sur le marché to issue shares

lancer un emprunt to issue a bond

langage boursier *m* Stock Market jargon

l/c (= Lettre de Crédit) *f* L/C

LCR (= Lettre de Change Relevé) *f* bills of exchange statement

légaliser une signature to authenticate a signature

légère baisse (des cours) *f* slight weakening (in prices)

législation financière *f* financial legislation

LEP (= Livret d'Épargne Populaire) *m* general savings account

lettre d'avis *f* advice note

lettre de change *f* bill of exchange, B/E

lettre de change relevé *f* bills of exchange statement

lettre de confirmation *f* letter of confirmation

lettre de confort *f* letter of comfort

lettre de crédit *f* letter of credit

lettre de crédit documentaire *f* documentary letter of credit

lettre de crédit irrévocable *f* irrevocable letter of credit

lettre de garantie *f* letter of guarantee

lettre de garantie bancaire *f* bank guarantee, banker's guarantee

lettre de relance des impayés *f* debt chasing letter

levée de fonds *f* raising of funds

levée des titres *f* taking delivery of shares

lever 10 milliards to pick up 10 billion

levier financier *m* financial leverage

libellé au porteur [*chèque*] made out to bearer

libellé en [*chèque*] made out in; [*cours*] quoted in, given in

libellé en dollars denominated in dollars

libeller to denominate; [*cheque*] to make out, to write

libeller à l'ordre de to make out to the order of, to make payable to

libération d'une action *f* paying up of a share

libérer entièrement des actions to make shares fully paid-up

libérer un débiteur to discharge a debtor

libre circulation des capitaux *f* free movement of capital

lieu d'émission *m* place of issue

lieu de paiement *m* place of payment

ligne magnétique *f* [*de carte bancaire*] magnetic stripe, black stripe

ligne de crédit *f* line of credit, credit line

ligne de découvert *f* overdraft facility

ligne de substitution *f* back-up line

limite à l'exercice *f* exercise limit

limite d'endettement *f* borrowing limit

limite de crédit *f* credit limit

limite de position *f* position limit

liquidateur *m* liquidator

liquidation *f* [*d'entreprise*] winding up, liquidation; [*de dette, compte*] settlement

liquidation d'une position *f* closing out of a position, liquidation of a position

liquidation de fin de mois *f* end of month settlement

liquidation de quinzaine *f* fortnightly settlement *Br*, half-monthly settlement

liquidation des biens *f* liquidation of assets

liquidation des opérations *f* settlement of trades, liquidation of trades

liquidation en espèces *f* cash settlement

liquide liquid

liquider une dette to pay off a debt

liquider une position to close out a position, to liquidate a position

liquidité *f* liquidity

liquidités *fpl* liquid assets

liste des tirages *f* list of drawings

livraison *f* delivery

livraison des titres *f* security delivery, delivery of securities

livre d'actionnaires *m* register of shareholders

livre de banque *m* bank ledger

livre de compte *m* account book

livrer to deliver

livres *mpl* [*d'une société*] books

livret A *m* "A" tax-free savings account with a savings ceiling

livret B *m* "B" taxable savings account with no ceiling

livret rose *m* savings account with higher interest rate for low earners

livret d'épargne populaire *m* general savings account

livret de caisse d'épargne *m* savings bank deposit book

LOA (= Location avec Option d'Achat) *f* lease with purchase option

location-bail *f* leasing

location simple *f* rental agreement

location de coffres *f* safe deposit box rental

lock box *m* safe deposit box

logo CB *m* banker's card logo

loi bancaire *f* banking law

loi Dailly *f* Dailly Act (simplified method of financing trade receivables)

loi Neiertz *f* Neiertz Act (law to prevent household indebtedness)

loi Scrivener *f* ≈ Consumer Credit Act

loi des finances *f* finance act

long terme *m* long term; *à long terme* long-term

lot *m* lot

louer [*locaux*] to rent, to lease *Am*; [*équipement*] to lease

loyer de l'argent *m* cost of money

M

M3 M3

mainteneur de marché *m* market maker

se **maintenir** [*cours de Bourse*] to hold up, to hold steady

maintien de cours: proposer un maintien de cours to make a standing offer to buy up all the shares at the price paid to acquire control of the company

maison d'acceptation *f* accepting house

maison de courtage *f* firm of brokers, brokerage house

maison de titres *f* securities house

majoration de prix *f* price mark-up

majorer to increase

mandataire *m* authorized signature

mandat général d'administration *m* discretionary management

mandat(-poste) *m* money order

manier de l'argent to handle money

manque à gagner *m* loss

manque à gagner potentiel *m* opportunity loss

manque de fonds *m* lack of funds

manque de provision *m* lack of funds

marchand de titres *m* dealer

marché *m* market; [*affaire, transaction*] deal

marché actions *m* securities market

marché baissier *m* bear market

marché boursier *m* Stock Market

marché continu *m* continuous market

marché domestique *m* domestic market

marché euro-obligataire *m* Eurobond market

marché extra-boursier *m* off-market

marché financier *m* financial market

marché financier européen *m* European financial market, Euromarket

marché gris *m* grey market

marché haussier *m* bull market

marché hors cote *m* unlisted market, over-the-counter market, OTC market

marché hypothécaire *m* mortgage market

marché immobilier *m* property market

marché interbancaire *m* interbank market

marché monétaire *m* money market

marché obligataire *m* bond market

marché ordonné *m* orderly market

marché organisé *m* regulated market

marché orienté à la baisse *m* bear market

marché orienté à la hausse *m* bull market

marché primaire *m* primary market

marché secondaire *m* secondary market

marché unique *m* single market

marché à règlement mensuel *m* monthly settlement market

marché à terme *m* futures market

Marché à terme international de France *m* French international financial futures exchange

marché au comptant *m* spot market

marché d'options négociables *m* traded options market

marché de bons à moyen terme *m* medium-term note market

marché de couverture *m* hedging market

marché de gré à gré entre banques *m* interbank wholesale market

marché de titres négociables *m* traded securities market

marché de l'Eurodevise *m* Euromarket

marché de l'occasion *m* secondary market

marché des actions *m* share market, equity market

marché des capitaux *m* capital market

marché des changes *m* foreign exchange market

marché des devises *m* currency market

marché des émissions *m* bond market

marché des nouvelles émissions *m* new issue market

marché des OAT *m* French government bond market

marché des obligations à long terme *m* long-term bond market

marché des titres *m* securities market

marché des titres négociables *m* traded securities market

marché des valeurs mobilières *m* share market, securities market

marché du neuf *m* primary market

marché du physique *m* physical market

marché entre banques *m* interbank market

marchéisation *f* marketization

marchés de capitaux *mpl* capital markets

marge *f* margin, variation margin

marge bancaire *f* banking margin

marge faible *f* thin margin

marge initiale *f* initial margin

marge d'intermédiation *f* interest margin

marge de crédit *f* credit margin

marge sur taux *f* interest rate spread; [*comptabilité*] net interest income

marketing bancaire *m* bank marketing

marketing financier *m* financial marketing

masse électronique *f* electronic transactions

masse monétaire *f* money supply

masse monétaire M3 *f* M3 money supply

masse papier *f* paper transactions

matières premières *fpl* commodities

Matif (= Marché À Terme International de France) *m* Matif

maturité *f* maturity; ***arriver à maturité*** to mature

mauvaise créance f bad debt

mécanisme de change m exchange rate mechanism, ERM

mécanisme de change européen m European exchange rate mechanism

mécanisme de financement m financing mechanism

membre de compensation m clearing member

membre de marché m market member

mensualiser to make payable by the month

mensualité f monthly instalment

mensuel monthly

mensuellement monthly

mercatique bancaire f bank marketing

messagerie f [*électronique*] electronic mail

méthode à échelles f daily balance interest calculation

méthode de financement f funding method

méthode par échelles f daily balance interest calculation

métier de banquier m banking profession, banking

mettre fin à sa position to close out one's position

milieux boursiers mpl Stock Exchange circles

milliard m billion, thousand million, (1,000,000,000)

millier m thousand

minimiser sa perte to minimize one's losses

ministère de l'Économie et des Finances m Treasury

ministère des Finances m Exchequer *Br*, Treasury Department *Am*

minoration f reduction

minorité de blocage f blocking minority vote

mise à disposition f [*de chéquiers*] issuing

mise de fonds f investment, outlay

mise en circulation f [*de billets*] issue

mise en demeure f formal notice; [*de paiement*] formal demand

mise en pension f borrowing against securities pledging

MLT (= Moyen, Long Terme) medium- to long-term

mobilisable [*créance*] discountable

mobilisation f raising

mobilisation de fonds f raising of funds

mobiliser [*créances*] to discount

mobiliser de l'argent to raise money

mobilité du capital f capital mobility

modalité d'amortissement f redemption method

modalité de paiement f method of payment

mode de règlement m method of payment

modèle de mathématique financière m mathematical financial model

moins less, minus

moins-value f capital loss

mois boursier m exchange month

mois d'échéance m trading month

mois d'expiration m expiry month

mois de livraison m delivery month

monde bancaire m banking world

mondialisation f globalization

mondialiser to globalize

MONEP (= Marché des Options NÉgociables à Paris) m MONEP

monétaire monetary
monétique *f* electronic money
monétisation *f* monetization
monétiser to monetize
monnaie *f* money; [*pièces*] change; [*devise*] currency
monnaie Banque de France *f* Bank of France funds
monnaie électronique *f* electronic money, electronic cash, e-money, e-cash
monnaie fiduciaire *f* paper money
monnaie forte *f* strong currency
monnaie internationale *f* international currency
monnaie locale *f* local currency
monnaie parallèle *f* parallel currency
monnaie scripturale *f* bank money, deposit money
monnaie unique *f* single currency
monnaie de compte *f* money of account
monnaie de papier *f* paper money
monnaie de réserve *f* reserve currency
monométallisme *m* monometallism
montant *m* amount
montant brut *m* gross amount, gross
montant dû *m* amount payable
montant maximum *m* maximum amount, maximum
montant minimum *m* minimum amount, minimum
montant net *m* net amount, net
montant total *m* total amount, total
monter en flèche to soar
mot de passe *m* password

mouvement ascensionnel *m* upward movement
mouvement boursier *m* Stock Market movement
mouvement d'un compte *m* account movement
mouvement de baisse *m* downward movement
mouvement de fonds *m* movement of funds
mouvement des capitaux *m* movement of capital
mouvement des cours *m* price fluctuation, price movement
mouvement des devises *m* currency fluctuation
mouvement des valeurs *m* share movements
mouvements monétaires *mpl* monetary fluctuations
moyen terme *m* medium term; *à moyen terme* medium-term
moyennant paiement in exchange for payment, subject to payment
moyenne *f* average; [*en statistique*] mean
moyens financiers *mpl* financial means
moyens liquides *mpl* liquid resources
moyens de paiement *mpl* means of payment
multibancarisation *f* growth in the number of banks
multidevise multicurrency
multirisques habitation *f* comprehensive household insurance
mutualisation des risques *f* mutualization of risk

N

nanti [*bien*] pledged
nantir (sur) to secure (on)
nantir des valeurs to deposit shares as security
nantissement *m* pledge, guarantee, security, collateral
nantissement "flottant" *m* floating charge
nantissement général *m* floating charge
nantissement subsidiaire *m* collateral security
nantissement de fonds de commerce *m* pledge over business assets, charge over business assets
négoce de titres *m* share dealing
négociabilité *f* negotiability
négociable negotiable, tradeable
négociateur *m* trader, dealer
négociateur individuel de parquet *m* local trader, local
négociation *f* trading, dealing
négociation de blocs d'actions *f* block trading
négociation entre courtiers *f* inter-dealer trading
négociations à prime *fpl* options trading
négociations à terme *fpl* futures trading
négociations au comptant *fpl* spot trading
négocier to trade, to deal

négocier à la criée to trade by open outcry
net net
net financier *m* net interest income; [*à payer*] net interest charges; [*prix net*] net price, net
niveau de clôture *m* closing level
niveau de dépôt requis *m* margin requirement
nominal nominal; par
nominal *m* [*d'action*] nominal value; [*d'obligation*] par value
non-admis à la cote unlisted
non à ordre not to order
non-bancaire non-bank
non-banque *f* non-bank
non dilué undiluted
non-ingérence *f* non-intervention
non-inscrit à la cote unquoted
non-paiement *m* non-payment
non-remboursement *m* non-repayment
non-valeur *f* [*créance*] worthless amount
normalisation *f* standardization
norme intersystème *f* inter-system standard
normes prudentielles *fpl* regulatory norms
normes de fonds propres *fpl* capital adequacy requirements
notation *f* rating
notation AAA *f* triple-A rating
noté triple "A" triple A rated

note de commission *f* commission note, fee note

note de crédit *f* credit note

note de débit *f* debit note

nouveaux emprunts *mpl* new borrowings

nouvel acheteur *m* first-time buyer

nouvel émetteur *m* new issuer

nouvelle émission *f* [*d'actions*] new issue

noyau dur *m* group of stable shareholders chosen for a company by the government on its flotation

nue-propriété *f* reversionary ownership

nul et non-applicable null and void

numéraire *m* cash

numéro confidentiel *m* [*de carte bancaire*] PIN, PIN number

numéro d'identité bancaire *m* bank sort code

numéro de carte *m* card number

numéro de compte *m* account number

nu-propriétaire *m* reversionary owner

O

OAT (= Obligation Assimilable du Trésor) *f* French government bond

obligataire *m* bondholder

obligataire *adj* debenture, bond

obligation *f* bond, debenture

obligation cautionnée *f* secured bond, custom-duty bill

obligation classique *f* straight bond

obligation convertible *f* convertible bond

obligation démembrée *f* stripped bond

obligation fictive *f* nominal bond

obligation garantie *f* guaranteed bond

obligation hypothécaire *f* mortgage bond

obligation indexée *f* index-linked bond

obligation la moins chère à livrer *f* cheapest deliverable bond

obligation nominative *f* registered bond

obligation très au-dessous du pair *f* deep discount bond

obligation à intérêt variable *f* floating rate bond

obligation à revenu fixe *f* fixed rate bond

obligation à revenu variable *f* floating rate bond

obligation à taux progressif *f* step-up bond

obligation à zéro coupon *f* zero-coupon bond

obligation au porteur *f* bearer bond

obligation de pacotille *f* junk bond

obligations *fpl* bonds, loan stock, loan notes

OBSA (= Obligation avec Bon de Souscription d'Actions) *f* bond with share warrant attached

obtention d'un prêt *f* obtaining of a loan

occasion de profit *f* profit opportunity

octroi *m* granting

octroi d'un prêt *m* granting of a loan

octroyer un prêt to grant a loan

offre *f* offer; [*dans appel d'offres*] bid; [*offre et demande*] supply

offre commerciale *f* bid

offre publique *f* takeover bid

offre publique d'achat *f* takeover bid

offre publique d'échange *f* takeover bid for shares

offre publique de vente *f* public offering, public share offer

offre de vente sans engagement *f* subject offer

oisif [*capital*] idle

OMCL (= Obligation la Moins Chère à Livrer) *f* cheapest delivrable bond

OPA (= Offre Publique d'Achat) *f* takeover bid; *être l'objet d'une OPA* to be the subject of a takeover bid

OPA amicale *f* friendly takeover bid

OPA inamicale *f* hostile takeover bid

OPA partielle *f* partial takeover bid

OPCVM (= Organisme de Placement Collectif en Valeurs Mobilières) *m* unit trust, UCITS, mutual fund *Am*

OPCVM actions *m* equity-based unit trust

OPCVM de court terme *m* short-term unit trust

OPE (= Offre Publique d'Échange) *f* takeover bid for shares

opéable ripe for takeover; *une société opéable* a prime takeover target

opeamania *f* takeover fever

opérateur *m* trader

opérateur principal de marché *m* primary dealer

opérateur en couverture *m* hedger

opérateurs de réseaux *mpl* network operators

opération *f* transaction

opération confirmée *f* matched trade

opération domestique *f* domestic transaction

opération financière *f* financial transaction

opération jumbo *f* jumbo trade

opération mixte *f* spread

opération scripturale *f* cash transaction

opération transfrontalière *f* cross-border trade

opération à la hausse *f* bull transaction

opération de change *f* foreign exchange trade

opération de journée *f* day trade

opération de masse *f* bulk transaction

opération en capital *f* capital transaction

opération sans détachement de droits *f* cum rights trade, transaction cum rights

opération sur titre *f* share deal

opérations fermes *fpl* firm transactions

opérations fictives *fpl* wash trading

opérations de Bourse *fpl* Stock Exchange transactions, share dealing

opérations de caisse *fpl* counter transactions

opérations en mode automatisé *fpl* computerized transactions

opérations sur blocs d'actions *fpl* block trading

opérations sur marge *fpl* margin trading

opérations sur le marché monétaire *fpl* money market transactions

opérer un virement to make a transfer

OPM (= Opérateur Principal de Marché) *m* primary dealer

opposition: faire opposition à un chèque to stop a cheque

optant *m* taker of an option

option *f* option

option américaine *f* American-style option

option asiatique *f* average rate option

option classique *f* traditional option

option couverte *f* covered option

option découverte *f* naked option

option européenne *f* European-style option

option ferme *f* firm option

option fille *f* underlying option

option mère *f* primary option

option négociable *f* traded option

option d'achat *f* option to buy; [*Bourse*] call option, call

option de change *f* foreign currency option

option de taux d'intérêt *f* interest rate option

option de vente *f* option to sell; [*Bourse*] put option, put

optionnaire *mf* granter of an option

option sur actions *f* option on shares

option sur indice *f* index option

option sur moyenne *f* average rate option

option sur option *f* compound option, option on an option

OPV (= Offre Publique de Vente) *f* public offering, public share offer

or *m* gold

or en barres *m* gold bullion, bullion

or en lingots *m* gold bullion, bullion

ORA (= Obligation Remboursable en Actions) *f* bond redeemable in shares

ordonnance de paiement *f* order to pay

ordonnancement *m* [*de paiement*] order to pay; [*mise en ordre*] scheduling

ordonnancer un paiement to order a payment, to authorize a payment

ordonnateur *m* payer; [*Bourse*] giver of an order

ordre *m* order; *à l'ordre de* payable to (the order of), to the order of

ordre conditionnel *m* contingent order

ordre environ *m* discretionary order

ordre exécution immédiate ou annulation *m* immediate or cancel order, fill or kill order

ordre ferme *m* firm order

ordre lié *m* contingent order

ordre limité *m* limit order

ordre stop *m* stop order

ordre stop à cours limité *m* stop-limit order

ordre "tout ou rien" *m* all-or-none order

ordre à cours limité *m* price limit order

ordre à exécution *m* open order

ordre à révocation *m* good-till-cancelled order

ordre à terme *m* futures order

ordre au comptant *m* cash order

ordre au cours *m* order at the prevailing price

ordre au dernier cours *m* order at the closing price

ordre au mieux *m* market order; *ordre aux mieux* at best order, at the market order

ordre d'achat *m* buy order, purchase order

ordre de détail *m* retail order

ordre de Bourse *m* Stock Exchange order

ordre de domiciliation *m* bank payment instructions form

ordre de négociation *m* trading order

ordre de paiement *m* payment order

ordre de prélèvement permanent *m* standing order

ordre de vente *m* order to sell, sell order

ordre de virement *m* transfer order

ordre par lots *m* block order

organisateur bancaire *m* bank administrator

organisation de cartes *f* card organization

organisme financier *m* financial institution

organisme prêteur *m* lender

organisme de compensation *m* clearing body

organisme de crédit *m* credit institution

organisme de placement collectif *m* investment fund

orientation de la Bourse *f* Stock Market trend

orienté à la baisse falling

orienté à la hausse rising

oscillation *f* [*d'une valeur*] fluctuation

osciller to fluctuate, to swing

OST (= Opérations Sur Titres) *fpl* securities dealing, securities trading

outil informatique *m* computing tool

outil de couverture *m* hedging instrument

outil de spéculation *m* trading instrument

ouverture d'un compte *f* opening of an account

ouverture d'une position *f* opening of a position

ouverture de crédit *f* granting of a loan

ouverture des marchés *f* opening up of markets
ouvrir un compte to open an account

ouvrir un crédit to grant a loan
ouvrir une position to open a position

P

PAJ (=Prêt Aidé à taux aJustable) *m* subsidized variable-rate mortgage
paiement *m* payment
paiement arriéré *m* payment in arrears
paiement comptant *m* cash payment
paiement électronique *m* electronic payment, payment by electronic transfer
paiement intégral *m* payment in full
paiement international *m* international payment
paiement transfrontière *m* cross-border payment
paiement transfrontière à distance *m* long-distance international payment
paiement transfrontière de proximité *m* short-distance international payment
paiement à échéance *m* payment at maturity

paiement à vue *m* payment at sight
paiement du solde *m* payment of the balance
paiement en espèces *m* cash payment
paiement par carte *m* card payment, payment by card
paiement par chèque *m* payment by cheque
paiements internationaux *mpl* international payments
pair *m* par; *au-dessus du pair* above par; *au pair* at par; *au-dessous du pair* below par
panier d'actions *m* basket of shares
panier de monnaies *m* basket of currencies
panique boursière *f* Stock Market panic
PAP (= Prêt d'Accession à la Propriété) *m* preferential rate mortgage
papier bancable *m* bankable paper

papier commercial *m* commercial paper

papier-monnaie *m* paper money

papier négociable *m* negotiable paper

papier à ordre *m* instrument to order

papier à vue *m* sight paper

papier au porteur *m* bearer paper

papiers valeurs *mpl* securities

paquet de valeurs *m* block of shares

paradis fiscal *m* tax haven

parc de comptes *m* account base

parité *f* parity; *au voisinage de la parité* close to par; *à parité* at the money

parité franc-mark *f* franc-mark parity

parité des monnaies *f* monetary parity

parités du change *fpl* exchange rate parity

parquet *m* [*de la Bourse*] floor, trading floor

participant de marché *m* market participant, player

passation d'un dividende *f* payment of a dividend

passation d'un ordre de Bourse *f* placing of an order on the Stock Exchange

passation de commande *f* placing of an order

passer commande à qn to place an order with sb

passer commande de qch to place an order for sth

passer un montant to post an amount

passif *m* liabilities

passif circulant *m* current liabilities

passif du bilan *m* liabilities

patrimoine *m* personal assets, net worth

patrimonial net worth

payable à l'échéance payable at maturity

payable à la banque payable at the bank

payable à terme échu payable in arrears

payable par anticipation payable in advance

payé d'avance prepaid, paid in advance

payer à vue to pay at sight

payeur *m* payer

payez au porteur pay to bearer

paysage bancaire *m* banking scene

PC (= Pièce de Caisse) *f* cash voucher

PEA (= Plan d'Épargne en Actions) *m* PEP

PEE (= Plan d'Épargne d'Entreprise) *m* company savings scheme

PEL (= Prêt Épargne Logement) *m* home loan savings account

pension *f* pension; [*titres*] repo; *mise en pension* borrowing against securities pledging

pension livrée *f* repo with actual delivery

pension de réversion *f* survivor's pension, reversionary pension

PEP (= Plan d'Épargne Populaire) *m* popular savings scheme

PER (= Plan d'Épargne de Retraite) *m* retirement savings scheme

perception *f* charge

perception à la source *f* tax deduction at source
perception de dividende *f* receipt of a dividend
percevoir [*commission, intérêts*] to receive
perdre sur to lose on
période de conversion *f* conversion period
période de récupération *f* payback period
période de référence *f* reference period
période de souscription *f* subscription period
personnel bancaire *m* banking staff
personnel de back-office *m* back-office staff
perte *f* loss; *à perte* at a loss
perte brute *f* gross loss
perte latente *f* unrealized loss
perte nette *f* net loss
perte potentielle *f* potential loss
perte d'intérêts *f* loss of interest
perte de bénéfice *f* loss of profit
perte de change *f* foreign exchange loss, exchange rate loss
perte de portage *f* carrying loss
perte en capitaux *f* capital loss
petit dépôt *m* retail deposit
petit porteur *m* small investor
pétro-dollar *m* petrodollar
peu liquide illiquid
phare *m* benchmark
PIB (= Produit Intérieur Brut) *m* GDP
PIBOR (= Paris InterBank Offered Rate) *m* PIBOR
PIBOR 3 mois *m* three-month PIBOR
pièce *f* coin

pièce de caisse *f* cash voucher
pièces en circulation *fpl* coins in circulation
pilotage *m* [*des marges d'intérêt*] management
place bancaire *f* banking centre
place boursière *f* stock market
place financière *f* financial centre, financial marketplace
place monétaire *f* money market
place off shore *f* offshore financial market
place de Paris *f* Paris market
placé en garantie pledged as security
placement *m* investment
placement avantageux *m* good investment
placement financier *m* financial investment
placement immobilier *m* property investment
placement obligataire *m* bond investment
placement à court terme *m* short-term investment
placement à long terme *m* long-term investment
placement à revenus fixes *m* fixed income investment
placement à revenus variables *m* variable income investment
placement en actions *m* share investment
placer [*ordre, titres*] to place; [*argent*] to invest
placer à court terme to invest short-term
plafond *m* ceiling
plafond d'autorisation *m* [*retrait d'argent avec CB*] withdrawal limit

plafond de découvert *m* overdraft limit

plafond de retrait *m* withdrawal limit

plafond du crédit *m* credit ceiling

plafonnement *m* levelling out

plafonner to level out, to level off; *être plafonné à* to have a ceiling of

plafonner réglementairement to put a regulatory limit on

plancher *m* [*d'un taux*] floor

plan d'épargne *m* savings plan

plan d'épargne-actions *m* personal equity plan

plan d'épargne-logement *m* saving scheme carrying a right to take out a mortgage loan

plan d'épargne populaire *m* popular savings scheme, 10 year scheme with savings ceiling and no tax after 8 years

plan d'épargne (de) retraite *m* retirement savings scheme

plan d'épargne d'entreprise *m* company savings scheme

plan d'épargne en actions *m* personal equity plan

plan de financement *m* funding plan, financial plan

plan de stock-options *m* stock-option programme

plomb *m* lead

plus-value *f* capital gain, increase in value, gain

PNB (= Produit National Brut) *m* GNP

point *m* point; *to rise/drop two points* gagner/perdre deux points

point argent *m* hole-in-the-wall machine, cashpoint

point mort *m* breakeven point

point de base *m* basis point

point de résistance *m* resistance level

point de l'or *m* price of gold

politique d'acquisitions *f* acquisitions policy

politique du crédit *f* credit policy

ponctionner des fonds to tap funds

pondération *f* weighting

pondérer to weight

pool bancaire *m* banking pool

portage *m* [*des titres, prêts, etc.*] carrying, piggy-backing

portage d'actions *m* carry

portefeuille diversifié *m* mixed portfolio

portefeuille-titres *m* share portfolio

portefeuille d'actions *m* share portfolio

portefeuille de titres *m* securities portfolio

porte-monnaie électronique *m* electronic wallet, electronic purse

porte-monnaie électronique rechargeable *m* refillable electronic wallet

se **porter acheteur** to be a buyer

se **porter caution pour qn** to stand surety for sb

se **porter garant envers** to stand surety for

porter intérêt to yield interest

porter un montant au crédit d'un compte to credit an amount to an account

porter un montant au débit d'un compte to debit an amount to an account

porter sur to have a lot size of

porteur *m* bearer

porteur d'actions *m* bearer of shares

porteurs d'emprunts russes *mpl* holders of Russian debt

porteur d'une traite *m* bearer of a bill

position *f* position; *en position courte* short; *être en position courte* to have a short position

position acheteur *f* long position

position courte assignée *f* assigned short position

position courte couverte *f* covered short position

position courte non couverte *f* uncovered short position

position couverte *f* covered position

position créditrice *f* credit balance

position débitrice *f* debit balance

position élémentaire *f* simple position

position financière *f* financial position

position globale *f* global position

position longue *f* long position

position non couverte *f* uncovered position

position ouverte *f* open position

position vendeur *f* short position

position d'un compte *f* balance of an account

possesseur de valeurs *m* share owner

poste *m* [*au bilan*] item

poste créditeur *m* credit item

poste débiteur *m* debit item

poste financier *m* financial item

post-marché *m* after-hours trading

pour cent per cent

pourcentage *m* percentage

pouvoyeur de capital-risque *m* venture capitalist

poussé par les profits profit-driven

pouvoir *m* [*procuration*] power of attorney

pouvoir d'achat *m* purchasing power

pratique bancaire *f* banking practice

préavis écrit *m* written advice

précompensation *f* pre-clearing

précontentieux *m* pre-litigation

prédateur *m* raider

prélèvement *m* debiting

prélèvement automatique *m* direct debit

prélèvement bancaire *m* direct debit

prélèvement libératoire *m* levy at source

prélever to withhold, to deduct

prélever une commission to deduct a commission

premier trimestre *m* first quarter

première de change *f* first of exchange

premium *m* premium

prendre à bail to take out a lease on, to lease

prendre son gain to take one's profit

prendre une position to take a position

preneur de lettre de change *m* payee of a bill of exchange

prépaiement *m* prepayment

prépayé prepaid

présentateur *adj* presenting

présentation à l'acceptation *f* presentation for acceptance

présentation au paiement *f* presentation for payment

présenter à l'encaissement to present for collection

presque banque *f* near bank
presse financière *f* financial press
pression à la vente *f* pressure to sell
prestataire non-banque *m* non-banking service provider
prêt *m* loan
prêt aidé à taux ajustable *m* subsidized variable rate mortgage
prêt bancaire *m* bank loan
prêt bonifié *m* soft loan
prêt conventionné *m* subsidized loan
prêt épargne logement *m* home loan savings account
prêt étudiant *m* student loan
prêt multidevise *m* multicurrency loan
prêt non garanti *m* unsecured loan
prêt participatif *m* equity loan
prêt personnalisé *m* personal loan
prêt personnel *m* personal loan
prêt-relais *m* bridging loan
prêt simple *m* simple credit
prêt à court terme *m* short-term loan
prêt à découvert *m* overdraft loan
prêt à intérêts *m* loan at interest
prêt à long terme *m* long-term loan
prêt à taux réduit *m* reduced rate loan
prêt à l'habitat *m* home loan
prêt en participation *m* syndicated loan
prêt en souffrance *m* non-performing loan
prêt sans intérêt *m* interest-free loan

prêt sur titres *m* loan against securities
prêter to lend
prêter à intérêt to lend at interest
prêter sur titres to lend against securities
prêteur *m* lender
prêteur *adj* lending
prête-nom *m* nominee company
prévision: en prévision de in the expectation of
prévoir [*hausse, baisse*] to forecast, to predict
prime *f* premium
prime d'émission *f* bond discount
prime de risque *f* danger money
principal *m* principal
principal et intérêts *m* principal and interest
principe mark to market *m* mark-to-market principle
prise ferme *f* bought deal; *syndicat de prise ferme* underwriting syndicate
prise de contrôle *f* takeover
prise de position *f* position taking
privilège de souscription *m* preferential subscription right
prix acheteur *m* bid price
prix boursier *m* exchange price
prix contractuel *m* contract price
prix ferme *m* firm price
prix plafond *m* upper price limit
prix vendeur *m* offer price
prix d'appel *m* loss-leading price
prix d'émission *m* issue price
prix d'exercice *m* [*d'option d'achat*] exercise price, strike price
prix de levée *m* exercise price, strike price

prix de négociation *m* trade price

prix de remboursement *m*
redemption price

procédure de livraison *f* delivery
procedure

prochain jour ouvrable *m* next
business day

productif d'intérêts interest-
bearing

produire des intérêts to bear
interest

produit bancaire *m* banking
product

produit dérivé *m* derivative

produit garanti *m* guaranteed-
income instrument, guaranteed
investment, no-loss investment

produit intérieur brut *m* gross
domestic product

produit national brut *m* gross
national product

produit net bancaire *m* net
banking revenue

produit obligataire *m* bond
instrument

produit patrimonial *m* asset
management product

produit d'épargne *m* savings
product

produit de financement *m*
financing product

produit de hors bilan *m* off-
balance sheet product

**produits assurance vie et
capitalisation** *mpl* life assurance
and savings products

produits financiers *mpl*
[*comptabilité*] interest income

profession bancaire *f* banking,
banking profession

**professionnels de l'analyse des
risques** *mpl* risk-analysis
professionals

profil patrimonial *m* personal
assets profile

profitable profitable

profondément hors des cours
deep out of the money

program trading *m* program
trading

**projet TBF (= Transferts
Banque de France)** *m* TBF
project

projet d'OPA (sur) *m* planned
takeover (of)

promoteur immobilier *m*
property developer

promotion immobilière *f* property
development

propriété immobilière *f*
property

proroger une échéance to extend
payment terms

prospectus *m* prospectus

protection achat carte *f* card
purchase insurance scheme

protection d'une position *f*
hedging of a position

protéger une position to hedge a
position

protestable protestable

protester [*un effet*] to protest

protêt *m* protest; *sans protêt*
without protest

provision *f* provision, cover

provision disponible *f* available
funds

provision insuffisante *f* [*sur un
compte*] insufficient funds

provision réglementée *f* special
tax allowance reserve

provision d'exploitation *f*
operating provision

**provision pour créances
douteuses** *f* provision for bad
debts

provision pour dépréciation *f* provision for depreciation
provisions sur risques-pays *fpl* provisions for country risk
provisionné [*compte*] in funds, in credit

provisionnement *m* funding
prudentiel prudential
purger une hypothèque to redeem a mortgage
put *m* put option, put

Q

quantité minimale *f* minimum quantity
quasi-monnaie *f* near money
quittance finale *f* final payment, final discharge
quittance pour solde de compte *f* closing account balance
quitte: être quitte d'une dette to be free of a debt
quote-part *f* share
quotité *f* lot
quotité de négociation *f* lot size

R

rachat *m* repurchase; [*de valeur, police, etc.*] redemption; [*de société*] buyout
rachat gagnant *m* repurchase at a profit
rachat d'entreprise par les salariés *m* management/ employee buyout

rachat d'entreprises à fort effet de levier *m* leveraged buy-out
rachetable [*action*] redeemable
racheter to buy back; [*dette, titres, etc.*] to redeem; [*entreprise*] to buy
racheter une obligation to retire a bond, to redeem a bond
racheteur *m* purchaser
radiation de la cote *f* delisting
radier de la cote to delist
raid *m* raid
raider *m* (corporate) raider
rally *m* rally
rapporter des intérêts to yield interest
rapprochement *m* reconciliation
rapprochement bancaire *m* bank reconciliation
raréfier [*une monnaie*] to restrict the supply of
rating *m* rating
ratio Cooke *m* Cooke ratio, risk asset ratio, capital adequacy ratio
ratio cours-bénéfice *m* price-earnings ratio
ratio réglementaire *m* regulatory ratio
ratio risque-rentabilité *m* risk-reward ratio
ratio d'endettement optimal *m* optimal debt (equity) ratio
ratio de couverture *m* hedge ratio
ratio de gestion *m* financial ratio, financial management ratio
ratio de liquidité *m* liquidity ratio
ratio de rentabilité *m* profitability ratio
ratio de situation *m* financial ratio
ratio de solvabilité *m* liquidity ratio
ratio de trésorerie *m* cash ratio

Rcb (= Réseau Cartes Bancaires) *m* banker's card network
réaliser [*valeur de qch*] to realize
réaliser des opérations to carry out transactions
réaliser un gain to make a profit
réaménager to reschedule
réassurance *f* reinsurance
réassurer to reinsure
réassureur *m* reinsurer
recapitalisation *f* recapitalization
réception *f* [*des dividendes, de l'intérêt*] receipt
récession *f* recession
recevoir un taux to receive a rate
recharger une carte to refill a card
réclamer le paiement to demand payment
reclassement de titres *m* secondary offering
reconductible renewable
reconduction *f* renewal
reconduire un bail to renew a lease
reconnaissance de dette *f* [*document*] debt instrument, IOU
recours *m* recourse
recouvrable [*dette*] recoverable, collectible
recouvrement de créances *m* debt collection
recouvrer [*créance, traite*] to collect
rectificatif *m* correction
recto *m* [*d'effet*] face
reçu *m* receipt
reculer [*cours de Bourse*] to drop
reculer un paiement to defer payment
récupérable recoverable
récupération *f* recovery
redressement *m* [*économique*] recovery

rééchelonnement *m* [*de dettes*] rescheduling

rééchelonner une dette to reschedule a debt

réescompte *m* rediscount; [*activité*] rediscounting

réescompter to rediscount

réévaluation *f* revaluation

réévaluer to revalue

réfaction *f* reduction

références bancaires *fpl* bank references, banker's references

références clients *fpl* client references

refinancement *m* [*d'un crédit*] refinancing

refinancer to refinance

refus de crédit *m* refusal of a loan

refus de paiement *m* non-payment; [*de traite*] dishonour

refuser un crédit to refuse a loan

régime de retraite *m* pension plan

régir des biens to manage assets

registre des actions *m* share register

registre du commerce *m* company register, Companies House *Br*

règlement *m* settlement; *au règlement* at settlement

règlement brut *m* gross settlement

règlement généré au fil de l'eau *m* continuously generated settlement

règlement instantané *m* instant(aneous) settlement

règlement net *m* net settlement

règlement à crédit *m* instalment payment

règlement au comptant *m* payment in cash

règlement des soldes *m* agreement of balances

règlement en temps réel *m* real-time settlement

règlement par chèque *m* payment by cheque

réglementaire regulatory

réglementation bancaire *f* banking regulations

réglementation de marché *f* market regulation

réglementation du change *f* exchange control regulations

régler [*fournisseur*] to pay; [*compte*] to settle

régler au comptant to pay in cash, to pay cash

règles de marché *fpl* market rules

règles de placement *fpl* investment regulations

regroupement *m* consolidation

régularisation *f* [*de comptes, stocks, charges*] adjustment

régulariser [*compte*] to adjust

régulateur bancaire *m* banking regulator

régulation *f* regulation

réinvestir to reinvest

rejet *m* [*d'un chèque*] refusal

rejeter [*chèque*] to refuse; *être rejeté* to bounce

relevé *m* statement

relevé bancaire *m* bank statement

relevé d'identité bancaire *m* bank details

relevé de compte *m* bank statement, statement of account

relevé de fin de mois *m* end-of-month statement

relever un compte to make out a statement of account

reliquat de compte *m* account balance

Relit *m* clearing system for share trading

remboursable repayable, refundable

remboursement *m* repayment, refund

remboursement anticipé *m* early redemption, early repayment

remboursement in fine *m* bullet repayment

rembourser to repay, to pay back, to refund

réméré *m* repo

remettre to remit

remettre un chèque to pay in a cheque

remettre une dette to waive a debt, to cancel a debt; [*à plus tard*] to defer (payment of) a debt

remettre à l'encaissement to send for collection

remettre à l'escompte to remit for discount

remise *f* [*rabais*] discount; [*de fonds*] remittance

remise à vue *f* demand deposit

remise d'effets *f* remittance of bills

remise d'une dette *f* cancellation of a debt; [*à plus tard*] deferment of (payment of) a debt

remise de fonds *f* remittance of funds

remisier *m* intermediate broker

rémunérateur [*placement*] interest-bearing, profitable

rémunération *f* payment

rémunération brute actuarielle *f* gross yield to redemption

rémunération de capital *f* interest on capital

rémunérer to pay

rendement *m* [*d'investissement*] return, yield; [*d'employé*] performance

rendement long *m* long-term yield

rendement moyen *m* average yield

rendement réel *m* actual yield

rendre 5% to yield 5%

renégociation *f* renegotiation

renégocier to renegotiate

renouvelable renewable

renouvelable automatiquement automatically renewable

renouveler [*crédit*] to roll over

renouveler un ordre to renew an order

renouveler une traite to renew a bill of exchange

renouvellement *m* renewal

renouvellement de carte bancaire *m* renewal of a bank card

renseignements de crédit *mpl* status enquiry, credit enquiry

rentabiliser des investissements to obtain a return on investments

rentabilité *f* profitability; [*d'investissement*] rate of return

rentabilité brute d'exploitation *f* gross operating profit

rentabilité nette d'exploitation *f* net operating profit

rentabilité du capital *f* return on capital

rentable profitable, cost-effective

rente *f* income

rente consolidée *f* consol

rente viagère *f* income for life

rentrer dans ses fonds to recoup one's investment

répartition des risques *f* risk spread

répartition du dividende *f* distribution of the dividend

replacement *m* reinvestment

report *m* [*à plus tard*] postponement, deferral; [*Bourse*] contango;

[*comptabilité*] carrying forward; *"report"* carried forward

report à nouveau carried forward

reports et avances sur titres *mpl* collateral loans

reporter une somme to carry a sum forward

représenter une traite à l'acceptation to re-present a bill for acceptance

reprise de provisions *f* recovery of provisions

reréglementation *f* reregulation

RES (= Rachat d'Entreprise par les Salariés) *m* MBO

réseau bancaire *m* banking network

réseau "Cartes Bancaires" *m* bank card network

réseau mutualiste *m* cooperative network

réseau de distribution *m* distribution network

réseau de guichets *m* branch network

Réserve fédérale *f* Federal Reserve

réserves *fpl* reserves

réserves obligatoires *fpl* compulsory reserves

réserves statutaires *fpl* statutory reserves, contractual reserves

réserves en devises *fpl* foreign currency reserves

réserves pour créances douteuses *fpl* doubtful debt provisions

résiliation *f* cancellation

responsable client *mf* account manager

responsable de salle de marché *mf* dealing room manager

responsable de sécurité *mf* security manager

responsable des engagements et des crédits *mf* credit manager

resserrement du crédit *m* credit squeeze

ressources financières *fpl* financial resources

ressources à long terme *fpl* long-term funds

restant de compte *m* account balance, account surplus

restructurer [*dette*] to restructure

résultat *m* result

résultat brut d'exploitation *m* gross operating profit

résultat conservé *m* retained earnings

résultat final *m* final balance

résultat financier *m* net interest income

résultat d'exploitation *m* operating profit

résultat de l'exercice *m* net profit after tax

retarder le paiement to delay payment

retenue à la source *f* deduction at source

retirer de l'argent to withdraw money

retirer de la circulation to withdraw from circulation

retirer sa participation d'une société to sell one's shares in a company, to sell out

retour de compensation *m* cleared funds

retour sur l'investissement *m* return on investment, ROI

retournement de marché *m* downturn in the market

retourner un effet to return a bill

se **rétracter** [*crédit*] to shrink

retrait *m* withdrawal

retrait automatique *m* automated withdrawal

retrait d'espèces *m* cash withdrawal

retraite *f* pension

retraite par capitalisation *f* funded pension scheme

rétrocession *f* retrocession

revaloriser to revalue

revendre to resell

revente simultanée *f* simultaneous resale

revenu *m* income

revenu imposable *m* taxable income

reverser une somme d'un compte sur un autre to transfer an amount from one account to another

réviseur interne *m* internal auditor

révision des limites de prix *f* revision of price limits

révocabilité *f* revocability

révocable [*crédit*] revocable, callable

RIB (= Relevé d'Identité Bancaire) *m* bank details, document giving bank details

RICE (= Relevé d'Identité Caisse d'Épargne) *m* savings bank account details

richesse *f* wealth

RIP (= Relevé d'Identité Postal) *m* post office account details

risque *m* risk, exposure

risqué risky

risque client *m* client risk, customer risk

risque illimité *m* unlimited risk

risque immobilier *m* property risk

risque limité *m* limited risk

risque-pays *m* country risk

risque privé *m* private risk

risque souverain *m* sovereign risk

risque tiré *m* drawee's risk

risque de baisse *m* downside risk

risque de change *m* foreign exchange risk

risque de contrepartie *m* counterparty risk

risque de conversion et de transfert *m* conversion and transfer risk

risque de crédit *m* credit risk

risque de hausse *m* upside risk

risque de marché *m* market risk

risque de signature *m* credit risk

risque de sortie anticipée *m* early exit risk

risque de spread *m* spread risk

risque de structure *m* structural risk

risque de taux d'intérêt *m* interest rate risk

risque de transfert *m* transfer risk

risque des cours *m* price risk

risque sur les entreprises *m* company risk

RM (= Règlement Mensuel) *m* monthly settlement

rompre un crédit avant son terme to foreclose on a loan

rompus *mpl* fractional rights

rouge: dans le rouge in the red; *passer dans le rouge* to go into the red

RR (= Rotation Rapide) *f* quick turnover

rupture abusive d'un crédit *f* irregular foreclosure on a loan

rythme de croissance *m* growth rate

S

SACI (= Société Anonyme de Crédit Immobilier) *f* home loan company

Sagittaire (= Système Automatique de Gestion Intégrée par Télétransmission de Transactions Avec Imputation de Règlements "Étranger") *m* automated system for overseas funds transfers

saisie-arrêt *f* garnishee order, attachment

saisie immobilière *f* seizure of property

salle de marchés *f* dealing room

salle des coffres-forts *f* vaults

salle des guichets *f* front office, banking hall

sans frais d'acquisition no-load

sans protêt without protest

sans valeur nominale no par value

satisfaire ses créanciers to satisfy one's creditors

Saturne (= Sytème Automatique de Traitement Unifié des Règlements de créances NÉgociables) *m* a system for clearing trade shares

sauf bonne fin subject to collection

sauvetage *m* rescue

SBF (= Sauf Bonne Fin) subject to collection

SCMC (= Société de Compensation des Marchés Conditionnels) *f* clearing house for MONEP

score *m* rating

SCPI (= Société Civile de Placement Immobilier) *f* property investment company

SCPI logements domestic property company

séance boursière *f* trading session

Sebc (= Système Européen des Banques Centrales) *m* European system of central banks

second marché *m* unlisted securities market, USM

secrétaire de banque *mf* banking secretary

secret bancaire *m* banking secrecy

secret professionnel *m* professional secrecy

sécuriser [*un financement*] to guarantee

sécurité *f* security

SEE (= Société des Emprunts Écureuil) *f* collective body in charge of bond issues for savings and providential institutions

semestriel half-yearly, semi-annual

série *f* series

série d'échéances *f* expiration series

série d'options *f* option series

service central des risques *m* central risk department (of the Bank of France)

service informatique *m* EDP department

service à la clientèle *m* customer service

service d'un emprunt *m* servicing a loan

service de transfert d'argent *m* money transfer service

service de la dette *m* debt servicing

service du change *m* foreign exchange department

service des titres *m* securities department

service des transferts *m* transfers department

services bancaires *mpl* banking services

services financiers *mpl* financial services

services de caisse *mpl* counter services

services de change *mpl* foreign exchange services

servir des intérêts to yield interest

servir une rente to pay an annuity

seuil d'annonce obligatoire *m* disclosure threshold

seuil de rentabilité *m* breakeven point

SICAF (= Société d'Investissement à CApital Fixe) *f* closed-end unit trust

SICAV (= Société d'Investissement à CApital Variable) *f* unit trust, mutual fund *Am*

SICAV actions *f* equity-based unit trust

SICAV court terme *f* short-term unit trust

SICAV diversifiée *f* diversified unit trust

SICAV monétaire *f* money unit trust

SICAV obligataire *f* bond-based unit trust

SICAV de trésorerie *f* money market fund

SICOMI (= Société Immobilière pour le COMmerce et l'Industrie) *f* property leasing company for industry and commerce

SICOVAM (= Société Interprofessionnelle de COmpensation de VAleurs Mobilières) *f* clearing house for share dealing

siège social *m* registered office, head office

signature autorisée *f* authorized signature

simulation personnalisée de prêt *f* personal loan sample presentation

sinistralité *f* rate of claims, claims experience

Sit (= Système Interbancaire de Télépaiement) *m* ≈ CHAPS *Br*, CHIPS *Am*

situation financière *f* financial situation

situation hebdomadaire *f* weekly return

situation mensuelle *f* monthly return

situation nette *f* net worth

situation de compte *f* account balance, account position

situation de la banque *f* bank balance, bank position

SME (= Système Monétaire Européen) *m* EMS

73

société anonyme de crédit immobilier *f* home loan company

société captive *f* captive company

société coopérative de banque *f* cooperative bank company

société emprunteuse *f* borrowing company

société financière *f* finance company

société holding *f* holding company

société immobilière *f* property company

Société immobilière pour le commerce et l'industrie *f* property leasing company for industry and commerce

société d'épargne *f* savings society

société d'investissements immobiliers *f* property investment trust, real estate investment trust

société d'investissement à capital fixe *f* closed-end unit trust

société d'investissement à capital variable *f* unit trust, mutual fund *Am*

société de Bourse *f* broker, securities house

société de capital-investissement *f* investment capital company

société de capital-risque *f* venture capital company

société de caution mutuelle *f* mutual guarantee insurance company

Société de compensation des marchés conditionnels *f* clearing house for MONEP

société de conseil en investissement *f* investment consultants

société de crédit immobilier *f* building society *Br*, savings & loan company *Am*

Société des Bourses françaises *f* Paris Bourse regulatory organization

solde *m* balance

solde actif *m* credit balance

solde bénéficiaire *m* credit balance

solde créditeur *m* credit balance

solde cumulé *m* cumulative balance

solde débiteur *m* debit balance

solde déficitaire *m* debit balance

solde disponible *m* available balance

solde immédiatement disponible *m* cleared balance

solde instantané *m* instant balance

solde moyen *m* average balance

solde passif *m* debit balance

solde réel *m* real balance, actual balance

solde de tout compte *m* final balance

solder un compte to balance an account

solidaire joint and several; *garant solidaire* joint and several garantor

solliciter un crédit to ask for a loan

solvabilité *f* credit-worthiness; *degré de solvabilité* credit rating

solvable credit-worthy

somme forfaitaire *f* lump sum

sommets et creux des cours *mpl* price highs and lows

Soréfi (= SOciété RÉgionale de FInance) *f* regional finance company

sortie *f* outflow

sorties de capitaux *fpl* outflows of capital

soulte *f* adjustment payment, balance payment

source de financement *f* source of finance

souscripteur *m* [*d'effet de commerce*] drawer; [*d'emprunt*] subscriber

souscription *f* subscription; [*garantie*] underwriting

souscrire to subscribe; [*garantir*] to underwrite

souscrire à des actions to subscribe for shares

souscrire un prêt to take out a loan; [*garantir*] to underwrite a loan

sous-participation *f* sub-participation

sous-total *m* subtotal

soustraire to subtract

soutenir le cours d'une monnaie to support a currency

spécialiste en valeurs du secteur public *mf* primary dealer in public sector shares

spécialiste en valeurs du Trésor *mf* primary dealer in government securities

spéculateur *m* speculator, trader

spéculateur à la baisse *m* bear

spéculateur à la hausse *m* bull

spéculateur sur variation minimale *m* scalper

spéculatif speculative

spéculation *f* speculation

spéculation à la baisse *f* bear trading

spéculation à la hausse *f* bull trading

spéculation sur les changes *f* speculation on the foreign exchange market

spéculer to speculate

spéculer à la baisse to go a bear, to be bearish

spéculer à la hausse to go a bull, to be bullish

sphères de la finance *fpl* financial circles

spot spot

spread baissier *m* bear spread

spread calendaire *m* time spread

spread diagonal *m* diagonal spread

spread haussier *m* bull spread

spread horizontal *m* horizontal spread

spread papillon *m* butterfly spread

stabilité des changes *f* exchange rate stability

stabilité des cours *f* price stability

stable stable

STAMP (= Système de Transactions Automatisé du MONEP) *m* MONEP automated trading system

statut bancaire *m* bank status

stellage *m* double option, straddle, put and call option

stochastique stochastic

stock d'encours *m* existing loan book

stop loss *m* stop loss limit

stratégie anti-OPA *f* anti-takeover strategy

stratégie de couverture *f* hedging strategy

stratégie de risques *f* risk management strategy

structure de financement *f* financing structure

succursale *f* branch

suivi de la clientèle *m* client monitoring

suivi des risques *m* risk monitoring

superbénéfice *m* superdividend plus directors' fees

superdividende *m* superdividend

support obligatoire *m* underlying bond

supprimer des crédits to cancel credits

surbancarisé overbanked

sur-coût *m* additional cost

sur-couverture *f* excess cover

surémission *f* over-issue

surendettement *m* over-indebtedness, over-gearing

sûreté en garantie d'une créance *f* surety for a loan

sur-offre *f* over-offering

surplus *m* surplus

sursis de paiement *m* extra time to pay

sursouscrit oversubscribed

surveillance des risques *f* risk monitoring

suspendre les paiements to stop payments, to suspend payment

suspension de paiements *f* moratorium on payment, stopping of payments

SVN (= Sans Valeur Nominale) NPV

SVP (= Spécialiste en Valeurs du secteur Publique) *m* primary dealer in public sector shares

SVT (= Spécialiste en Valeurs du Trésor) *m* primary dealer in government securities

swap *m* swap

swap vanilla *m* vanilla swap

swap de change *m* exchange rate swap

swap(p)er to swap

syndicat bancaire international *m* international banking syndicate

syndicat financier *m* financial syndicate

syndicat d'émission *m* underwriting syndicate

syndicat de banquiers *m* banking syndicate

syndicat de bonne fin *m* underwriting syndicate

syndicat de prise ferme *m* underwriting syndicate

syndication *f* syndication

système électronique de paiement *m* electronic payment system

système européen des banques centrales *m* European system of central banks

système extra-boursier de cotation des titres *m* off-exchange quotation system

système interbancaire de télécompensation *m* interbank computerized clearing system

Système monétaire européen *m* European Monetary System

système monétaire international *m* international monetary system

système d'aide à la décision *m* decision support system

système de compensation interbancaire *m* interbank clearing system

système de contrôle des changes *m* exchange control system

système de cotation *m* quotation system

système de criée *m* open outcry system

système de paiement *m* payment system

système de place *m* trading system

système de règlement livraison *m* settlement and delivery system

système de règlements *m* settlement system

système de retraite *m* pension scheme

système de transfert de fonds électronique *m* electronic funds transfer system, EFTS

T

Tabac (To "Automated clearing house" By Automated Correspondent) ≈ CHAPS *Br*, CHIPS *Am*

tableau de financement *m* cashflow statement

tableur *m* spreadsheet

taille boursière *f* market size

talon *m* [*de chèque*] stub, counterfoil

TAM (= Taux Annuel Monétaire) *m* annual monetary benchmark rate

tantième *m* percentage

tarif *m* [*prix*] rate

tarifaire tariff

tarifer to set the rate of

tarification *f* setting of rates

tassement des actions *m* fall in share prices

taux *m* rate

taux actuariel *m* yield to redemption

taux annuel glissant *m* year-on-year rate

taux bancaire *m* bank rate

taux court *m* short-term rate, short rate

taux court monétaire *m* short-term money rate

taux dégressif *m* tapering rate

taux directeur *m* key rate

taux effectif global *m* annual percentage rate, APR

taux facial *m* face value

taux fixe *m* fixed rate; *à taux fixe* fixed-rate

taux forfaitaire *m* flat rate

taux hybride *m* hybrid rate

taux interbancaire *m* interbank rate

taux interbanque offert *m* Interbank Offered Rate

taux interne de rentabilité *m* internal rate of return

taux Lombard *m* Lombard rate

taux long *m* long-term rate, long rate

taux long obligataire *m* long-term bond rate

taux minima *mpl* minimum rates

taux moyen du marché monétaire *m* average money market rate

taux nominal *m* nominal rate

taux officiel *m* official rate

taux pivot *m* central rate

taux plafond *m* cap

taux plancher *m* floor

taux préférentiel *m* prime rate

taux privé *m* market rate

taux proportionnel *m* proportional interest rate

taux réduit *m* reduced rate

taux réel *m* real rate

taux uniforme *m* uniform rate, flat rate

taux variable *m* variable rate; *à taux variable* variable-rate

taux variable monétaire *m* variable monetary rate

taux variable obligataire *m* variable bond rate

taux à court terme *m* short-term rate

taux à long terme *m* long-term rate

taux d'actualisation *m* discount rate (for calculating NPV)

taux d'appel d'offre *m* intervention rate

taux d'échange *m* rate of exchange, exchange rate

taux d'épargne *m* savings rate

taux d'escompte *m* discount rate

taux d'inflation *m* inflation rate

taux d'intérêt *m* interest rate, rate of interest

taux d'intérêt contractuel *m* contractual interest rate

taux d'intérêt nominal *m* nominal interest rate

taux d'intérêt réel *m* real interest rate

taux d'intérêt à long terme *m* long-term interest rate

taux d'intervention *m* intervention rate

taux d'usure *m* penal rate

taux de base *m* base rate

taux de base bancaire *m* bank base rate

taux de change *m* exchange rate, rate of exchange

taux de conversion *m* conversion rate

taux de défaillance *m* default rate

taux de marché monétaire *m* money market rate

taux de placement *m* investment rate

taux de prise en pension *m* repo rate

taux de rendement *m* rate of return

taux de référence *m* benchmark rate, reference rate

taux de refinancement *m* refinance rate

taux de rendement actuariel *m* yield to redemption

taux de replacement *m* reinvestment rate

taux de rotation *m* turnover rate

taux de transformation *m* [*assurance*] conversion rate

taux de l'argent au jour le jour *m* overnight rate, call rate

taux de l'intérêt *mpl* interest rates

taux de l'usure *m* usury rate

taux de la prime *m* premium rate

taux des fonds fédéraux américains *m* (American) Federal Funds rate

taux des repos *m* repo rate

taux du change *m* exchange rate

taux du coupon *m* coupon rate

taxe à la valeur ajoutée *f* value-added tax

TBB (= Taux de Base Bancaire) *m* base rate, bank base rate

TBF (= Transferts Banque de France) *mpl* French automated clearing system

TEG (= Taux Effectif Global) *m* APR

télématique *f* electronic data transmission

téléscripteur *m* ticker tape, ticker

télétransmission *f* computerized transmission

temps réel: en temps réel in real time

tendance ascensionnelle *f* upward trend

tendance haussière *f* upward trend

tendance à la baisse *f* downward trend

teneur du marché *m* market maker

tenir à bail to hold a lease on

tenir un compte chez to bank with, to have an account with

tenue de la Bourse *f* state of the market

terme: à terme forward; *acheter à terme* to buy forward; *à terme échu* on the due date; *à terme fixe* fixed-term; *à très court terme* very short-term

terme d'échéance *m* [*d'effet*] maturity date

terme de liquidation *m* account period, settlement period

terminal électronique *m* electronic terminal

terminal électronique de paiement *m* electronic payment terminal

terminal multi-fonction *m* multi-function terminal

terminal point de vente *m* point of sale terminal

TF (= Taux Fixe) *m* fixed rate

thêta *m* theta

tiers porteur *m* [*d'effet*] holder in due course

TIO (= Taux Interbanque Offert) *m* IBOR

TIOP (= Taux Interbancaire Offert à Paris) *m* PIBOR

tirage *m* [*de chèque*] drawing; [*de prêt*] drawdown

tirage au sort *m* drawing (for bonds to be redeemed)

tiré *m* drawee

tiré par la demande demand-led

tirer to draw; *tirer un chèque/une traite sur* to draw a cheque/a bill on

tirer à courte échéance to draw a short-dated bill

tirer à découvert to overdraw, to overdraw one's account

tirer à vue to draw at sight

tireur *m* drawer

titre *m* security

titre long *m* long bond

titre négociable *m* negotiable instrument

titre nominatif *m* registered security

titre participatif *m* equity loan

titre universel de paiement *m* universal payment order

titre à courte échéance *m* short-dated security

titre à échéance fixe *m* dated security

titre à longue échéance *m* long-dated security

titre à revenu fixe *m* fixed income security

titre à revenu variable *m* floating rate security

titre à terme *m* future

titre au porteur *m* bearer bond

titre d'action *m* share certificate

titre d'obligation *m* loan note, bond note

titre de créance *m* loan note, debt instrument

titre de créance négociable *m* marketable security, negotiable debt instrument

titre de dette avec coupons *m* coupon-bearing strip

titre de dette synthétique sans coupon *m* zero-coupon strip

titre de participation *m* equity investment

titre de propriété *m* title deed

titre de rente *m* government bond

titres *mpl* securities, stock *Am*

titres déposés en nantissement *mpl* securities lodged as collateral

titres émis *mpl* issued securities

titres libérés *mpl* fully paid-up securities

titres participatifs *mpl* equity loan issue

titres de placement *mpl* marketable securities

titrisation *f* securitization

titriser to securitize

titulaire *mf* holder

titulaire d'actions *mf* shareholder

titulaire de carte *mf* cardholder

titulaire de compte *mf* account holder

TJJ (= Taux de l'argent au Jour le Jour) *m* overnight rate, call rate

T4M (= Taux Moyen Mensuel du Marché Monétaire au jour le jour) *m* average monthly rate of the overnight money market rate

TME (= Taux de rendement Moyen mensuel des Emprunts d'État) *m* average monthly government bond yield

TMM (= Taux de Marché Monétaire) *m* money market rate

TMP (= Taux Moyen Pondéré du marché au jour le jour) *m* weighted average rate of the overnight money market

tontine *f* tontine

tontinier tontine

total général *m* grand total

totaliser to total

toucher un chèque to cash a cheque

toucher un intérêt to receive interest

TP (= Titres Participatifs) *mpl* equity loan issue

TPV (= Terminal Point de Vente) *m* POS terminal

TR (= Taux Réglementé) *m* statutory rate

trader *m* trader

traite *f* draft; [*lettre de change*] bill of exchange

traite bancaire *f* bank draft

traite documentaire *f* documentary bill

traite pro forma *f* pro forma bill

traite à courte échéance *f* short-dated bill

traite à date fixe *f* time bill

traite à longue échéance *f* long-dated bill

traite à vue *f* sight draft

traite contre acceptation *f* acceptance bill

traite de complaisance *f* accommodation bill

traite "sans frais" *f* bill "without protest"

traitement transactionnel *m* processing of transactions

traitement de comptes *m* account processing

traitement des chèques *m* cheque processing

traitements au fil de l'eau *mpl* continuous processing, ongoing processing

traitements de masse *mpl* bulk processing

traiter des opérations de banque to transact banking business

traiter un chèque to process a cheque

tranche *f* tranche

tranche de paiement *f* instalment

transaction *f* transaction; [*boursier*] trade, transaction

transaction valeur jour *f* value today trade

transaction au comptant *f* spot transaction

transaction de clôture *f* closing trade

transaction en devises *f* currency transaction

transaction par carte *f* card transaction

transactions bancaires *fpl* bank transactions

transactions boursières *fpl* Stock Exchange transactions

transférable transferable

transfert bancaire *m* bank transfer

transfert électronique de fonds *m* electronic funds transfer

transfert d'actions *m* transfer of shares

transfert de capitaux *m* transfer of capital, capital transfer

transfert de devises *m* currency transfer

transfert de fonds *m* transfer of funds

transfert de fonds électronique à partir du point de vente *m* electronic funds transfer at the point-of-sale, EFTPOS

transfert par CCP *m* giro transfer

transfrontières cross-border

transmissible par endossement transferable by endorsement

transmission par endossement *f* transfer by endorsement

Trésor *m* Treasury

Trésor public *m* Treasury Department

trésorerie aisée *f* improved cashflow

trésorerie nette *f* net cash position

trésorier *m* treasurer

trésorier de banque *m* bank treasurer

trimestre *m* quarter

trimestriel quarterly

troncation *f* [*dématérialisation*] truncation

trust bancaire *m* banking trust

TSDI (= Titres Subordonnés à Durée Indéterminée) *mpl* perpetual subordinated loan stock

tunnel *m* [*options*] collar

TUP (= Titre Universel de Paiement) *m* universal payment order

TVA (= Taxe à la Valeur Ajoutée) *f* VAT

TVM (= Taux Variable Monétaire) *m* variable monetary rate

TVO (= Taux Variable Obligatoire) *m* variable bond rate

U

UEM (= Union Économique et Monétaire) *f* EMU

Union économique et monétaire *f* Economic and Monetary Union

Union Européenne Monétaire *f* European Monetary Union

union monétaire à deux vitesses *f* two-speed monetary union

unité monétaire *f* monetary unit

unité de compte *f* unit of account

unité de transaction *f* lot size

unité de l'action sous-jacente *f* unit of the underlying instrument

Unitime *m* Unitime

usages bancaires *mpl* banking practices

utilisable [*crédit*] available

utilisation frauduleuse *f* fraudulent use

V

vaciller [*d'une monnaie*] to be unsteady, to wobble

valable valid

valeur *f* [*de qch*] value; [*titre, etc.*] security

valeur actuelle nette *f* net present value

valeur bilantielle *f* book value

valeur boursière *f* market value

valeur ce jour *f* value today

valeur cotée *f* quoted security

valeur étrangère *f* foreign security

valeur faciale *f* face value

valeur intrinsèque *f* intrinsic value

valeur jour *f* same-day value

valeur juste *f* [*d'une option*] fair value

valeur liquidative *f* close-out value, settlement value

valeur mobilière *f* security

valeur mobilière de placement *f* marketable security

valeur négociable *f* marketable security

valeur nominale *f* [*d'une obligation*] par value; [*d'une action*] nominal value

valeur nominative *f* registered security

valeur non cotée *f* unlisted security

valeur réalisable *f* realizable security, marketable security

valeur refuge *f* safe investment

valeur spéculative *f* speculative security

valeur temporelle *f* time value

valeur transactionnelle *f* settlement value

valeur vedette *f* blue chip stock

valeur vénale *f* fair market value

valeur à revenu fixe *f* fixed interest security, fixed income security

valeur à revenu variable *f* variable rate security, floating rate security

valeur à l'échéance *f* maturity value

valeur à l'encaissement *f* value for collection

valeur de Bourse *f* quoted security

valeur de père de famille *f* blue chip, gilt-edged stock

valeur de placement *f* marketable security

valeur de premier ordre *f* blue chip

valeur de spéculation *f* speculative value; [*titre, etc.*] speculative security

valeur du second marché *f* unlisted security

valeur en Bourse *f* Stock Market value

valeurs admises au règlement mensuel *fpl* shares quoted on the monthly settlement market

valeurs cotées *fpl* listed stock,

quoted securities

valeurs disponibles *fpl* marketable securities

valeurs émises *fpl* securities issued

valeurs des sociétés industrielles *fpl* industrials

validation au fil de l'eau *f* continuous validation, ongoing validation

valider [*un règlement*] to validate

valoir to be worth

valorisation *f* valuation

valorisation au prix de marché *f* [*d'options*] marking to market

valorisé [*capital*] with interest

valoriser to value

VAN (= Valeur Actuelle Nette) *f* NPV

variable *f* variable; *à revenu variable* variable-rate, variable-yield

variation annuelle *f* annual change

variations de prix *fpl* price fluctuations, price variations

vecteur *m* vector

vega *m* vega

véhicule d'investissement immobilier *m* property investment instrument

veille de l'échéance *f* day before maturity

velléités de baisse des taux *fpl* slight fall in prices

vendeur *m* seller; *se porter vendeur* to be a seller

vendre to sell

vendre à découvert to sell short

vendre à terme to sell forward

vendre au comptant to sell for cash

vente *f* sale

vente ferme *f* firm sale

vente nue *f* naked sale

vente sèche *f* uncovered sale

vente à découvert *f* short sale

vérification (comptable) *f* audit

vérification à rebours *f* audit trail

vérifier to verify; [*comptes*] to audit

versement *m* payment; [*partiel*] instalment; [*à la banque*] deposit

versement partiel *m* instalment

versements échelonnés *mpl* staggered payments

verser to pay; [*à la banque*] to deposit, to pay in

verser entièrement [*actions*] to fully pay up

verser qch au crédit de qn to credit sb with sth

verso d'un chèque *m* back of a cheque

virement *m* transfer

virement automatique *m* standing order

virement bancaire *m* bank transfer

virement interbancaire *m* interbank transfer

virement postal *m* post office transfer

virement SWIFT *m* SWIFT transfer

virement par courrier *m* mail transfer

virement par télex *m* telex transfer

virer to transfer

viser un effet to stamp a bill

visibilité à moyen terme *f* medium-term visibility

vitesse de circulation *f* circulation rate

VMP (= Valeurs Mobilières de Placement) *fpl* marketable securities

volatil volatile
volatilité *f* volatility
volatilité implicite *f* implied
  volatility
volatilité des marchés *f* market
  volatility, volatility of the
markets
volatilité des taux *f* rate volatility
volume des transactions *m*
  transaction volume, volume of
  trading
vue: à vue at sight; [*dépôt*] demand

warrant *m* warrant
warrant découvert *m* naked
  warrant
zinc *m* zinc
zinzins *mpl* [*investisseurs
  institutionnels*] institutional
investors
zone dollar *f* dollar area
zone monétaire *f* monetary area
zone de parités fixes *f* fixed-parity
  area

A

to **abandon at expiry** abandonner à l'échéance

abandonment at expiry abandon à l'échéance *m*

to **absorb debts** éponger des dettes

accelerated depreciation amortissement dégressif *m*

acceptance acceptation *f*

acceptance bill traite contre acceptation *f*

acceptance credit crédit par acceptation *m*

acceptance fee commission d'acceptation *f*

acceptance house maison d'acceptation *f*

accepting house maison d'acceptation *f*

Access® carte Eurocard Mastercard® *f*

access: to have access to finance accéder à des financements

to **access the market** aborder le marché

accommodation bill traite de complaisance *f*

account compte *m*; *to have an account with* avoir un compte en banque à; *account in credit* compte créditeur *m*; *account in debit* compte débiteur *m*

account balance reliquat de compte *m*; [*surplus*] restant de compte *m*; [*position*] situation de compte *f*

account commission commission de compte *f*

account credit avoir de compte *m*

account day jour de liquidation *m*

account executive chargé de clientèle *m*

account fee commission de compte *f*

account handling fee commission de tenue de compte *f*

account holder détenteur d'un compte *m*, titulaire de compte *mf*

account management charge frais de tenue de compte *mpl*

account management fee frais de tenue de compte *mpl*

account manager chargé de compte *m*, responsable client *mf*

account movement mouvement d'un compte *m*

account number numéro de compte *m*

account payable compte créditeur *m*, dette fournisseur *f*

account payee only à porter en compte

account period terme de liquidation *m*

account position situation de compte *f*

account processing traitement de comptes *m*

account receivable compte

87

débiteur *m*, créance client *f*
account surplus restant de compte *m*
accountant comptable *mf*
accounting comptabilité *f*
accounting day journée comptable *f*
accounting year année comptable *f*
accounts [*accounting*] comptabilité *f*; [*records*] écritures *fpl*, comptes *mpl*
accounts analysis analyse des comptes *f*
accounts clerk aide-comptable *mf*
accrued dividends dividendes accrus *mpl*
accrued interest intérêt couru *m*, intérêts échus *mpl*
accruing interest intérêts à échoir *mpl*
ACH (= **Automated Clearing House**) chambre de compensation automatisée *f*
acquisition acquisition *f*
acquisitions policy politique d'acquisitions *f*
active portfolio management gestion active de portefeuille *f*
actual balance solde réel *m*
actual yield rendement réel *m*
actuarial actuariel
actuary actuaire *mf*
to **add up to** se chiffrer à
adding up chiffrage *m*
additional cost sur-coût *m*
adjudication in bankruptcy jugement déclaratif de faillite *m*
to **adjust** [*account*] régulariser
adjustment régularisation *f*, ajustement *m*
adjustment account compte collectif *m*

administration charge frais d'administration *mpl*
administration fee frais de dossier *mpl*
administrative costs frais d'administration *mpl*
administrator [*in bankruptcy*] administrateur (judiciaire) *m*
admission to the Stock Exchange List admission à la cote *f*
advance avance (de fonds) *f*; [*down payment*] acompte *m*
advance against income avance sur recettes *f*
advice note avis *m*, lettre d'avis *f*
advising bank banque notificatrice *f*
affiliated affilié
to **affix one's signature** apposer sa signature
after-hours trading post-marché *m*
agency bank antenne de banque étrangère *f*
agency fee commission de gestion *f*
agent bank banque mandataire *f*
to **agree on a price** s'entendre sur un prix
agreement of balances règlement des soldes *m*
to **allocate** allouer
to **allocate funds to** affecter des fonds à
allocation allocation *f*
all-or-none order ordre "tout ou rien" *m*
to **allot** [*shares*] attribuer
allotment [*of shares*] attribution *f*
allowance [*against tax*] abattement *m*
American dollar dollar américain *m*

assets

American Fed(eral) Funds fonds
fédéraux américains *mpl*
American Federal Funds rate
taux des fonds fédéraux
américains *m*
American-style option option
américaine *f*
amortization amortissement *m*
amortization of expenditure
amortissement-dépenses *m*
to amortize amortir
amount montant *m*
amount payable montant dû *m*
analysis analyse *f*
analyst analyste *mf*
annual change variation
annuelle *f*
annual depreciation annuité
d'amortissement *f*
annual fee cotisation annuelle *f*
annual interest intérêt annuel *m*
annual (general) meeting
assemblée générale (ordinaire) *f*
annual percentage rate taux
effectif global *m*
annual writedown annuité
d'amortissement *f*
annualized percentage rate taux
effectif global *m*
annuity annuité *f*
annuity flow flux d'annuités *m*
annuity purchase constitution de
rente *f*
to antedate antidater
to anticipate an increase
escompter une hausse
anti-inflation(ary) anti-
inflationniste
antiraid precautions barrières
antiraid *fpl*
anti-takeover strategy stratégie
anti-OPA *f*
Apacs (= Association for

PAyment Clearing Services)
association de services de
compensation *f*
application right droit de
souscription *m*
to apply for a loan demander un
prêt
to apply for a share souscrire une
action
to appreciate [*currency*]
s'apprécier
appreciation appréciation *f*;
*appreciation of the franc
against the mark* appréciation
du franc contre le mark
APR (= Annual Percentage Rate)
TEG *m*, taux effectif global *m*
arb (= arbitrageur) arbitragiste *m*
arbitrage arbitrage *m*
arbitrageur arbitragiste *m*
arbitraging arbitrage *m*
armed security escort convoyeur
de fonds *m*
arrangement fee [*for overdraft*]
commission d'ouverture de
crédit *f*
to ask for a loan solliciter un crédit
ask price prix demandé *m*, cours
vendeur *m*
asset depreciation dépréciation
d'actif *f*
asset management gestion
d'actifs *f*, gestion de
patrimoine *f*
asset management product
produit patrimonial *m*
asset manager gestionnaire de
patrimoine *mf*
asset portfolio portefeuille des
actifs *m*
asset quality qualité des actifs *f*
asset risk risque des actifs *m*
assets actif du bilan *m*

to **asset-strip** [*company*] démembrer

asset-stripping démembrement *m*, réalisation de l'actif suite au rachat d'une société *f*

assigned short position position courte assignée *f*

assignee cessionnaire *mf*

assignment cession *f*, assignation *f*

assignment of a debt délégation d'une dette *f*

assignment of debtors délégation d'une dette *f*

assignment of loans délégation de crédits *f*

assistant accountant aide-comptable *mf*

ATM (= Automatic Teller Machine) *Am* DAB *m*, distributeur automatique de billets *m*

to **attach conditions** afficher des conditions

attachment [*of salary, etc.*] saisie-arrêt *f*

attested certifié

audit contrôle de comptes *m*, vérification (comptable) *f*

to **audit** [*accounts*] apurer

audit committee comité d'audit *m*

audit trail vérification à rebours *f*

auditing apurement *m*

auditor auditeur *m*, contrôleur *m*

to **authenticate a signature** légaliser une signature

authorization [*for payment*] autorisation *f*

authorization slip fiche d'autorisation *f*

authorized accrédité, habilité

authorized overdraft découvert autorisé *m*

authorized overdraft facility encours débiteur autorisé *m*

authorized signatory mandataire *mf*

authorized signature signature autorisée *f*

authorized to sign habilité à signer

autobank distributeur automatique de billets *m*

to **automate** automatiser

automated banking automatisme bancaire *m*

automated clearing house chambre de compensation automatisée *f*

automated payment virement automatique *m*

automated transaction transaction automatique *f*

automated withdrawal retrait automatique *m*

automatic cash dispenser distributeur automatique de billets *m*

automatic exercise exercice automatique *m*

automatic teller machine *Am* distributeur automatique de billets *m*

automatically renewable renouvelable automatiquement

automation automatisation *f*

available disponible

available balance solde disponible *m*

available capital capitaux disponibles *mpl*

available credit crédit disponible *m*

available funds provision disponible *f*

aval aval bancaire *m*

to **avalize** avaliser

average moyenne *f*
average balance solde moyen *m*
average money market rate taux moyen du marché monétaire *m*

average movement flux moyen *m*
average rate option option sur moyenne *f*, option asiatique *f*
average yield rendement moyen *m*

B

back [*of a cheque*] verso *m*
to **backdate** antidater
back-dated rétroactif
back-end costs [*for fund*] frais de sortie *mpl*
back interest arrérages *mpl*, intérêts arriérés *mpl*
back-load fees [*for fund*] frais de sortie *mpl*
back office back-office *m*
back office staff personnel de back-office *m*
back to back credit crédit back to back *m*
back-up line ligne de substitution *f*
backer bailleur de fonds *m*
backwardation déport *m*
BACS (= Bankers' Automated Clearing System) système de télépaiement *m*; *to pay by BACS* payer par EDI
bad debt créance douteuse *f*
bad debts encours douteux *mpl*
bad loan write-off passation par

pertes d'une créance impayée *f*, abandon de créance *m*
balance solde *m*; [*after audit*] reliquat *m*; [*remaining amount*] restant *m*; [*situation, state*] situation *f*
to **balance** équilibrer; *to balance an account* solder un compte
balance forward [*on bank statement*] report de solde *m*
balance of payments balance des paiements *f*
balance sheet bilan (comptable) *m*
balance-sheet *adj* bilantiel
balloon solde de remboursement *m*
bancassurance bancassurance *f*
bank banque *f*
bank *adj* bancaire
to **bank with** tenir un compte chez
bank acceptance acceptation de banque *f*
bank account compte en banque *m*
bank accountancy comptabilité de banque *f*

bank accountant comptable (de banque) *mf*

bank accounting comptabilité bancaire *f*

bank administrator organisateur bancaire *m*

bank advice avis de la banque *m*

bank balance situation de compte *f*

bank balance sheet bilan bancaire *m*

bank base rate taux de base bancaire *m*, TBB *m*

bank bill *Am* billet de banque *m*

bank book journal de banque *m*

bank borrowings emprunts bancaires *mpl*

bank branch filiale de banque *f*, agence bancaire *f*

bank branch code code guichet *m*

bank card network réseau cartes bancaires *m*

bank charges frais bancaires *mpl*, agios *mpl*, agios bancaires *mpl*

bank cheque chèque bancaire *m*, chèque de banque *m*

bank clerk employé de banque *m*, guichetier *m*

bank commission commission bancaire *f*

bank counter guichet de banque *m*

bank credit [*assets*] avoir en banque *m*

bank customers clientèle bancaire *f*

bank debt [*owed to banks*] créance bancaire *f*

bank default défaillance bancaire *f*

bank deposit dépôt bancaire *m*

bank details relevé d'identité bancaire *m*, RIB *m*

bank discount rate escompte officiel *m*

bank draft traite bancaire *f*

bank employee employé de banque *m*

bank fee commission bancaire *f*

bank finance financement bancaire *m*

bank float flottant bancaire *m*

Bank for International Settlements Banque de Règlements Internationaux *f*

bank funding financement bancaire *m*

bank giro slip ordre de virement *m*

bank guarantee garantie bancaire *f*, lettre de garantie bancaire *f*

bank holiday jour férié *m*

bank interest intérêt bancaire *m*

bank ledger livre de banque *m*

bank lending concours bancaire *m*

bank loan prêt bancaire *m*, crédit bancaire *m*

bank manager directeur de banque *m*

bank marketing marketing bancaire *m*

bank money monnaie scripturale *f*

bank note billet de banque *m*

bank notification avis de la banque *m*

Bank of England Banque d'Angleterre *f*

Bank of England funds monnaie Banque d'Angleterre *f*

Bank of France Banque de France *f*

bank overdraft découvert bancaire *m*

bank position situation de la banque *f*

bank rate taux bancaire *m*
bank reconciliation rapprochement bancaire *m*
bank references références bancaires *fpl*
bank sort code code banque *m*
bank statement relevé bancaire *m*, relevé de compte *m*
bank status statut bancaire *m*
bank supervisor surveillant bancaire *m*
bank teller guichetier *m*
bank transactions transactions bancaires *fpl*
bank transfer transfert bancaire *m*, virement bancaire *m*
bank transfer advice avis de virement *m*
bank treasurer trésorier de banque *m*
bankable paper papier bancable *m*
banker banquier *m*
banker's acceptance acceptation bancaire *f*
banker's card carte bancaire *f*
banker's draft chèque de banque *m*
banker's guarantee garantie bancaire *f*, lettre de garantie bancaire *f*
banker's references références bancaires *fpl*
banking banque *f*
banking *adj* bancaire
banking and finance group groupe bancaire et financier *m*
banking association association bancaire *f*
banking business activité bancaire *f*
banking centre place bancaire *f*
Banking Commission Commission bancaire *f*

banking consortium consortium de banques *m*
banking controls contrôle bancaire *m*
banking customers clientèle bancaire *f*
banking day jour ouvrable *m*
banking economics économie bancaire *f*
banking environment environnement bancaire *m*
banking group groupe bancaire *m*
banking hall salle des guichets *f*
banking hours heures d'ouverture des banques *fpl*
banking intermediary intermédiaire bancaire *m*
banking law loi bancaire *f*; [*as subject*] droit bancaire *m*
banking lawyer juriste de banque *m*
banking margin marge bancaire *f*
bank marketing mercatique bancaire *f*
banking network réseau bancaire *m*
banking operative exploitant de banque *m*
banking pool pool bancaire *m*
banking practice pratique bancaire *f*
banking practices usages bancaires *mpl*
banking product produit bancaire *m*
banking profession profession bancaire *f*
banking regulations réglementation bancaire *f*
banking regulator régulateur bancaire *m*
banking scene paysage bancaire *m*

banking secrecy secret bancaire *m*

banking sector secteur bancaire *m*, exploitation bancaire *f*

banking services services bancaires *mpl*

banking staff personnel bancaire *m*

banking syndicate syndicat de banquiers *m*

banking terms conditions de banque *fpl*

banking trust trust bancaire *m*

banking world monde bancaire *m*

bankrupt failli *m*; *to go bankrupt* faire faillite; *to be bankrupt* être en faillite

bankruptcy faillite *f*; [*criminal*] banqueroute *f*

base lending rate taux de base bancaire *m*

base rate taux de base bancaire *m*, TBB *m*

basis point point de base *m*

basis (rate) swap swap de tarifs de base *m*, échange de taux de référence *m*

basket of currencies panier de monnaies *m*

basket of shares panier d'actions *m*

bear spéculateur à la baisse *m*; *to go a bear* spéculer à la baisse

bear *adj* [*market*] baissier

to **bear**: *to bear interest* produire des intérêts; *to bear the costs* assumer les frais

bear market marché baissier *m*, marché orienté à la baisse *m*

bear spread spread baissier *m*

bear trading spéculation à la baisse *f*

bearer porteur *m*

bearer bill effet au porteur *m*

bearer bond obligation au porteur *f*, titre au porteur *m*

bearer cheque chèque au porteur *m*

bearer instrument instrument au porteur *m*

bearer of a bill porteur d'une traite *m*

bearer of shares porteur d'actions *m*

bearer paper papier au porteur *m*

bearer share action au porteur *f*

bearish baissier; *to be bearish* spéculer à la baisse

bed and breakfast [*shares selling*] manœuvre consistant à vendre des titres avec possibilité de rachat ultérieur à des fins fiscales *f*

benchmark référence *f*, phare *m*

benchmark government bond emprunt d'État de référence *m*

benchmark rate taux de référence *m*

beneficiary accrédité *m*, bénéficiaire *mf*

best: at best order ordre au mieux

bid offre *f*; [*in tender*] soumission *f*

to **bid** offrir; *22 bid, 23 offered* cours acheteur 22, cours vendeur 23

bid price cours acheteur *m*, prix offert *m*, prix acheteur *m*

Big Bang [*on London Stock Exchange*] déréglementation de la bourse de Londres *f*

big bank grande banque *f*, enseigne bancaire *f*

big investor grand investisseur *m*

bill [*instrument*] effet *m*; [*Am: banknote*] billet de banque *m*; [*invoice*] facture *f*

bill for collection effet à
l'encaissement *m*

bill made out to bearer effet au
porteur *m*

bill of exchange effet de change
m, lettre de change *f*

bill without protest effet sans
protêt *m*, traite sans frais *f*

billing facturation *f*

billion (1,000,000,000) milliard *m*

**BIS (= Bank for International
Settlements)** BRI *f*

black knight chevalier noir *m*

black stripe [*on credit card*] ligne
magnétique *f*

blank cheque chèque en blanc *m*

blank draft effet en blanc *m*

to **blank endorse** endosser en
blanc

to **block** [*funds*] bloquer

block of shares bloc d'actions *m*,
paquet de valeurs *m*

block order ordre par lots *m*

block trade achat en bloc *m*

block trading opérations sur blocs
d'actions *fpl*, négociation de
blocs d'actions *f*

blocked cheque chèque bloqué *m*

blocking [*of prices, salaries*]
blocage *m*

blocking minority vote minorité
de blocage *f*

blue book blue book *m*

blue chip valeur de père de famille
f, valeur de premier ordre *f*

blue chip company entreprise de
premier plan *f*

blue chip stock valeur vedette *f*

bond obligation *f*

bond discount prime d'émission *f*

bondholder détenteur
d'obligations *m*, obligataire *mf*

bond instrument produit

obligataire *m*

bond investment placement
obligataire *m*

bond issue émission d'obligations
f, emprunt obligataire *m*; *to
make a bond issue* émettre un
emprunt obligataire

bond market marché obligataire
m, marché des émissions *m*

bonus issue émission d'actions
gratuites *f*

bonus share action gratuite *f*

book entry securities titres
dématérialisés *mpl*

book value valeur bilantielle *f*

book-keeping entries écritures
comptables *fpl*

books livres *mpl*

boom boom *m*

to **borrow** emprunter; *to borrow
money from* emprunter de
l'argent à

to **borrow against** emprunter sur

borrower emprunteur *m*

borrowing emprunt *m*

borrowing *adj* emprunteur

borrowing capacity capacité à
emprunter *f*, capacité
d'endettement *f*

borrowing company société
emprunteuse *f*

borrowing facility facilité
d'emprunt *f*

borrowing limit limite
d'endettement *f*

borrowing rate taux d'emprunt *m*

bought deal achat ferme *m*, prise
ferme *f*

to **bounce** être rejeté; *chèque
which bounces* chèque en
bois *m*

branch succursale *f*, agence *f*,
guichet *m*

branch manager directeur d'agence *m*, directeur de succursale *m*

branch network réseau de guichets *m*

brassplate centre centre boîte aux lettres *m*

to **break down** [*figures*] ventiler

to **break through the (107) barrier** franchir la barre (de 107)

breakdown of charges décompte d'agios *m*

breakeven point seuil de rentabilité *m*, point mort *m*

bridging loan prêt-relais *m*, crédit-relais *m*

broken interest intérêts intérimaires *mpl*

broker courtier *m*, agent de change *m*; [*company*] société de Bourse *f*; **firm of brokers** maison de courtage *f*

broker-dealer courtier-marchand de titres *m*

brokerage courtage *m*

brokerage fee droit de courtage *m*, commission de courtage *f*

brokerage house maison de courtage *f*

broking house maison de courtage *f*

bubble [*financial*] bulle *f*

buck dollar américain *m*

budget card carte de crédit avec approvisionnement mensuel fixe du compte *f*

building society société de crédit immobilier *f*, caisse d'épargne-logement *f*

building society account plan d'épargne-logement *m*

bulk processing traitements de masse *mpl*

bulk transaction opération de masse *f*

bull spéculateur à la hausse *m*; **to go a bull** spéculer à la hausse

bull *adj* haussier

bull market marché haussier *m*, marché orienté à la hausse *m*

bull spread spread haussier *m*

bull trade jeu à la hausse *m*

bull trading spéculation à la hausse *f*

bull transaction opération à la hausse *f*

bulldog bond obligation étrangère libellée en sterling *f*

bullet in fine

bullet repayment amortissement in fine *m*, remboursement in fine *m*

bullion or en barres *m*

bullish haussier; **to be bullish** spéculer à la hausse

buoyancy dynamisme *m*

buoyant [*market*] dynamique, porteur

bureau de change bureau de change *m*

business affaires *fpl*; [*company*] entreprise *f*

business day jour ouvrable *m*

business deposit dépôt entreprises *m*

business loans crédit aux entreprises *m*

butterfly spread spread papillon *m*

to **buy** acheter

to **buy back** racheter

to **buy for cash** acheter au comptant

to **buy forward** acheter à terme

to **buy on margin** acheter sur marge

buyback rachat *m*

buyback right droit de rachat *m*

buy contract contrat d'achat *m*

buy note contrat d'achat *m*

buy order ordre d'achat *m*, injonction à l'achat *f*

buyout rachat *m*

buyer acheteur *m*; *to be a buyer* se porter acheteur

buyer credit crédit-acheteur *m*

C

CA (= Chartered Accountant) expert-comptable *m*

C/A (= Current Account) CCB *m*, C/C *m*

CAC 40 index indice CAC 40 *m*

calendar year année civile *f*

call appel *m*; *at call* [*money*] à vue; *call francs put dollars* call francs put dollars *m*

to **call in** [*loan*] demander le remboursement de

call deposit dépôt à vue *m*

call for capital appel de fonds *m*

call money argent au jour le jour *m*

call of twice more option d'achat doublée à la hausse *f*

call option call *m*, option d'achat *f*

call rate taux de l'argent au jour le jour *m*, TJJ *m*

callable loan crédit révocable *m*

called-up capital capital appelé *m*

to **cancel** annuler, résilier; [*debt*] remettre

to **cancel credits** dénoncer des crédits, supprimer des crédits

cancellation annulation *f*, résiliation *f*; [*of debt*] remise *f*

cancellation clause clause d'annulation *f*, clause de résiliation *f*

cap taux plafond *m*

capital capital *m*, capitaux *mpl*

capital adequacy normes de fonds propres *fpl*

capital adequacy ratio ratio Cooke *m*, ratio de solvabilité *m*

capital adequacy requirements [*of BIS*] normes de fonds propres *fpl*

capital assets actif immobilisé *m*

capital base fonds propres *mpl*

capital control contrôle des capitaux *m*

capital employed capital engagé *m*

capital gain plus-value *f*
capital gains tax impôt sur la
   plus-value *m*
capital guarantee garantie du
   capital *f*
capital investment investissement
   de capitaux *m*
capital loss perte en capitaux *f*,
   moins-value *f*
capital market marché des
   capitaux *m*
capital markets marchés de
   capitaux *mpl*
capital mobility mobilité du
   capital *f*
capital revenue collecte de
   capitaux *f*
capital transaction opération en
   capital *f*
capital transfer transfert de
   capitaux *m*
capital transfer tax taxe sur le
   transfert de capitaux *f*
capitalization capitalisation *f*
to **capitalize** capitaliser
capitalized and bad debts
   créances immobilisées et
   douteuses *fpl*
captive company société captive *f*
**CAR (= Compounded Annual
   Rate)** taux annuel composé *m*
car insurance assurance auto *f*
car loan crédit auto *m*
card carte *f*
card issuer émetteur de cartes *m*
card organization organisation de
   cartes *f*
card payment paiement par
   carte *m*
card purchase insurance scheme
   protection achat carte *f*
card transaction transaction par
   carte *f*

carried forward report, report à
   nouveau
carry portage d'actions *m*
to **carry a sum forward** reporter
   une somme
carrying portage *m*
carrying cost coût de portage *m*
carrying gain gain de portage *m*
carrying loss perte de portage *f*
cash espèces *fpl*, numéraire *m*,
   (argent) liquide *m*; [*item on
   balance sheet*] caisse *f*; *to pay
   cash* payer (au) comptant; *for
   cash* au comptant
to **cash a cheque** toucher un
   chèque
cash advance avance de
   trésorerie *f*
cash and bullion encaisse
   métallique *f*
cash assets actifs liquides *mpl*
cash card carte de retrait
   d'espèces *f*
cash deficit déficit de trésorerie *m*
cash deposit dépôt d'espèces *m*
cashdesk caisse *f*
cash dispenser distributeur
   automatique *m*
cash facilities crédit de
   trésorerie *m*
cash facility facilité de caisse *f*
cashflow trésorerie *f*
cashflow difficulties difficultés de
   trésorerie *fpl*
cashflow from operations
   excédent de trésorerie
   d'exploitation *m*, ETE *m*
cashflow management gestion de
   la trésorerie *f*
cashflow statement tableau de
   financement *m*
cash holdings disponibilités *fpl*
cash in till encaisse *f*

cash machine distributeur de billets *m*

cash management gestion de la trésorerie *f*, gestion des liquidités *f*

cash on hand espèces en caisse *fpl*

cash on hand and at bank disponibilités en caisse et en banque *fpl*

cash order ordre au comptant *m*

cash payment paiement comptant *m*, paiement en espèces *m*

cashpoint point argent *m*, distributeur de billets *m*

cashpoint card carte de retrait d'espèces *f*

cashpoint machine distributeur de billets *m*, point argent *m*

cashpoint withdrawal retrait automatique *m*

cash purchase achat au comptant *m*

cash ratio ratio de trésorerie *m*

cash reserves réserves en espèces *fpl*, disponibilités *fpl*

cash settlement liquidation en espèces *f*

cash shortage insuffisance de trésorerie *f*

cash statement bordereau de caisse *m*

cash surplus excès de trésorerie *m*

cash transaction opération scripturale *f*

cash voucher pièce de caisse *f*, PC *f*

cash withdrawal retrait d'espèces *m*, décaissement *m*

cashable encaissable

cashier caissier *m*

cashier's check *Am* chèque de banque *m*

CD (= Certificate of Deposit) CD *m*

CD (= Cash Dispenser) DAB *m*

ceiling plafond *m*; *to have a ceiling of* être plafonné à

central account compte centralisateur *m*

central bank banque centrale *f*

central banker banquier central *m*

central clearing house centre d'échange des opérations à compensation *m*, CEC *m*

central rate taux pivot *m*

certificate of deposit certificat de dépôt *m*

certificate of investment certificat d'investissement *m*

certified cheque chèque certifié *m*

certified public account *Am* expert-comptable *m*

CGT (= Capital Gains Tax) impôt sur la plus-value *m*

CHAPS (= Clearing House Automated Payment System) ≈ Sit *m*

charge perception *f*, agio *m*; *charge to* imputation à *f*

to **charge sth to sth** imputer qch sur qch; *to charge sth to sb* imputer qch à qn; *charge it to my account* mettez cela sur mon compte

charge card carte de paiement *f*, carte privative *f*

charge over business assets nantissement de fonds de commerce *m*

charge over property gage immobilier *m*

chargeable imputable; *to be chargeable to* être à la charge de

charging date date de valeur *f*

chartered accountant expert-comptable *m*

chartism analyse Chartiste *f*
chartist analyste graphique *mf*
check [*of documents, etc.*] contrôle *m*; *Am* chèque *m*
checkbook *Am* carnet de chèques *m*, chéquier *m*
checking account *Am* compte chèque *m*, compte courant *m*
cheque chèque *m*
chequebook carnet de chèques *m*, chéquier *m*
cheque-clearing compensation de chèques *f*
cheque form formule de chèque *f*
cheque guarantee card carte bancaire *f* (*indispensable pour payer par chèque*)
cheque made out to bearer chèque au porteur *m*
cheque made out to name chèque nominatif *m*
cheque No. CH No, chèque numéro
cheque processing traitement des chèques *m*
chief accountant chef comptable *m*
Chinese wall cloisonnement entre activités financières *m*
CHIPS (= Clearing House Interbank Payment System) *Am* ≈ Sit *m*
circulation: in circulation [*coins, money, etc.*] en circulation
circulation of capital circulation des capitaux *f*
circulation of currency circulation des devises *f*
circulation of finance circuits de financement *mpl*
circulation of funds circulation des flux *f*
circulation of money circulation monétaire *f*

circulation rate vitesse de circulation *f*
CIRCUS (= Combined Interest Rate and CUrrency Swap) échange de taux sur devises *m*
city: the City la City
city analyst analyste financier *m*
claims experience [*of insurer*] sinistralité *f*
to **clear** compenser; *to be cleared at* être compensable à
clear day jour franc *m*
clearance [*of cheque*] compensation *f*
cleared balance solde immédiatement disponible *m*
cleared cheque chèque compensé *m*
cleared funds fonds compensés *mpl*, retour de compensation *m*
clearer banque compensatrice *f*
clearing [*of cheque*] compensation *f*
clearing account compte de compensation *m*
clearing agreement accord de compensation *m*, accord de clearing *m*
clearing bank banque compensatrice *f*, banque de dépôts *f*
clearing body organisme de compensation *m*
clearing cycle circuit de compensation *m*
clearing fees frais de compensation *mpl*
clearing house chambre de compensation *f*
clearing member adhérent-compensateur *m*, intermédiaire compensateur *m*
clearing price cours de

compensation *m*

clearing system système de compensation *m*

client file fichier client *m*

client references références clients *fpl*

client risk risque client *m*

client risk management gestion du risque client *f*

close of trading clôture *f*

to **close** *vi* [*of Stock Market*] clôturer

to **close a deal** arrêter un marché

to **close an account** [*at bank*] clore un compte, fermer un compte; [*in accounting*] arrêter un compte

to **close at a loss** clôturer à perte

to **close off an account** arrêter un compte

to **close out** dénouer

to **close (out) a position** fermer une position, clore une position, liquider une position

close-out value valeur liquidative *f*

closed-end unit trust société d'investissement à capital fixe *f*, SICAF *f*

closing fermeture *f*; [*of Stock Market*] clôture *f*

closing account balance quittance pour solde de compte *f*

closing date [*for share offer*] date de clôture *f*

closing level niveau de clôture *m*

closing of an account clôture de compte *f*, fermeture d'un compte *f*

closing out of a position clôture d'une position *f*, liquidation d'une position *f*

closing price cours de clôture *m*, cote de clôture *f*

closing time heure de fermeture *f*

closing trade transaction de clôture *f*

closure by repurchase clôture par rachat *f*

closure of a position fermeture de position *f*

co-borrower co-emprunteur *m*

co-financing co-financement *m*

coin pièce *f*; *coins in circulation* pièces en circulation

collar [*for options*] tunnel *m*

collateral nantissement *m*

collateral loans reports et avances sur titres *mpl*

collateral security nantissement subsidiaire *m*

collateralization collatéralisation *f*

to **collateralize** garantir

to **collect** [*debts*] recouvrer; [*taxes*] percevoir; [*bill, cheque*] encaisser

collection [*of debts*] recouvrement *m*; [*of taxes*] perception *f*; [*of bill, cheque*] encaissement *m*; *to send a cheque for collection* remettre un chèque à l'encaissement

collection charge commission d'encaissement *f*, commission de paiement *f*

collection fee commission d'encaissement *f*, commission de paiement *f*

combination of positions combinaison de positions *f*

combined interest rate and currency swap échange de taux sur devises *m*

commercial bank banque commerciale *f*

commercial banking banque commerciale *f*

commercial bill effet de
commerce *m*

commercial credit crédit
commercial *m*

commercial customer client
commercial *m*

commercial debt créance
commerciale *f*

commercial deed acte
commercial *m*

commercial loan prêt
commercial *m*

commercial paper billets de
trésorerie *mpl*

commercial property immobilier
d'entreprise *m*

commercial transactions
échanges commerciaux *mpl*

commission commission *f*

commission costs frais de
commission *mpl*

commission note note de
commission *f*

commitment [*undertaken by a
bank*] engagement *m*; *without
commitment* sans
engagement *m*

commitment fee commission
d'engagement *f*

commodities matières
premières *fpl*

commodities exchange Bourse de
commerce *f*

commodity dealer courtier en
matières premières *m*

company cheque chèque
d'entreprise *m*

company risk risque sur les
entreprises *m*

compensable indemnisable

to **compensate** indemniser; *to
compensate sb for sth*
indemniser qn de qch

compensation [*act*] indemnisation
f; [*money received*] indemnité *f*

competitive advantage avantage
concurrentiel *m*

complaints manager inspecteur
chargé des réclamations *m*

composite index indice
composite *m*

composite rate taux composite *m*

compound interest intérêt
composé *m*, intérêts
composés *mpl*

compound option option sur
option *f*

compounded annual rate taux
annuel composé *m*

comprehensive insurance
assurance multirisque *f*,
assurance tous risques *f*

Comptroller of the Currency *Am*
contrôleur de la monnaie *m*

computer crime criminalité
informatique *f*

computerization
informatisation *f*

to **computerize** informatiser

computerized banking
informatique bancaire *f*

computerized accounts
comptabilité informatisée *f*

computerized transactions
opérations informatisées *fpl*

computerized transmission
télétransmission *f*

computing tool outil
informatique *m*

concert party action de concert *f*

conditions of execution
conditions d'exécution *fpl*

confirmation commission
commission de confirmation *f*

confirmation fee commission de
confirmation *f*

confirmation of execution
confirmation d'exécution *f*
confirmed credit crédit
confirmé *m*
confirming bank banque
confirmatrice *f*
consideration contrepartie *f*
consol rente consolidée *f*
to **consolidate a debt** consolider
une dette
consolidated debt dette
consolidée *f*
consolidation consolidation *f*
consols consolidés *mpl*
consortium bank banque
consortiale *f*
consumer borrowing crédit à la
consommation *m*
consumer credit crédit à la
consommation *m*
Consumer Credit Act ≈ loi
Scrivener *f*
consumer credit loan prêt de
crédit à la consommation *m*
consumerist consumériste
contango report *m*
contested debt créance litigieuse *f*
contingent order ordre
conditionnel *m*, ordre lié *m*
**continuous automated trading
system** cotation assistée en
continu *f*
continuous market marché
continu *m*
contract contrat *m*
contract note avis
d'exécution *m*, avis d'opération
sur titre *m*
contract price prix contractuel *m*
contractual interest rate taux
d'intérêt contractuel *m*
contractual reserves réserves
statutaires *fpl*

to **contribute** cotiser
controlling interest bloc de
contrôle *m*
conversion and transfer risk
risque de conversion et de
transfert *m*
conversion date date de
conversion *f*
conversion of loan notes/stock
conversion d'un emprunt *f*
conversion period période de
conversion *f*
conversion rate taux de
conversion *m*; [*insurance*] taux
de transformation *m*
to **convert loan notes/stock**
convertir un emprunt
to **convert securities** convertir des
valeurs
convertibility
convertibilité *f*
convertible convertible
convertible bond obligation
convertible *f*
convertible loan stock emprunt
obligataire convertible *m*
convertible share action
convertible *f*
Cooke ratio ratio Cooke *m*
cooperative bank banque
coopérative *f*, banque
mutualiste *f*
cooperative network réseau
mutualiste *m*
copper cuivre *m*
corporate banking banque
d'entreprise *f*
corporate client entreprise-
cliente *f*
corporate finance ingénierie
financière *f*
corporate lending crédit aux
entreprises *m*

corporate lending department
direction clientèle
entreprises *f*

corporate raider attaquant *m*,
raider *m*

correspondent bank banque
correspondante *f*

correspondent bank account
compte de correspondant *m*

co-signatory cosignataire *mf*

cost coût *m*

cost centre centre d'analyse *m*

cost hedging couverture des
frais *f*

cost of money loyer de l'argent *m*

cost overrun dépassement de
coût *m*

cost-push inflation inflation par
les coûts *f*

costs incurred frais encourus *mpl*

to **count** compter

counter guichet *m*; *over the
counter market* marché hors
cote *m*

counter clerk guichetier *m*

counter services services de
caisse *mpl*

counter transactions opérations
de caisse *fpl*

counterfoil talon *m*

counter-guarantee contre-
garantie *f*

counterparty contrepartie *f*; *as
counterparty* en contrepartie

counterparty risk risque de
contrepartie *m*

to **countersign** contresigner

countertrade commerce
d'échange *m*

countervalue contrevaleur *f*

counting comptage *m*

country risk risque-pays *m*

coupon coupon *m*

coupon-bearing strip titre de
dette avec coupons *m*

coupon rate taux du coupon *m*

cover provision *f*

to **cover** couvrir

to **cover a loss** couvrir un déficit

to **cover an overdraft** couvrir un
découvert

to **cover one's exposure** couvrir
les engagements

covered call call couvert *m*

covered option option couverte *f*

covered position position
couverte *f*

covered short position position
courte couverte *f*

covered writer [*of options*]
émetteur couvert *m*

**CPA (= Certified Public
Accountant)** *Am* expert-
comptable *m*

crash krach *m*

to **create a hedge** constituer une
couverture

to **create a mortgage** constituer
une hypothèque

creation of a mortgage
constitution d'hypothèque *f*

credit crédit *m*; *to buy on credit*
acheter à crédit; *to be in credit*
être créditeur

to **credit** créditer; *to credit an
account* créditer un compte; *to
credit an amount to an account*
créditer une somme sur un
compte; *to credit sb with sth*
verser qch au crédit de qn; *in
credit* provisionné

credit account compte créditeur *m*

credit advice avis de crédit *m*, avis
de réception de fonds *m*

credit agreement convention de
crédit *f*

credit application demande d'ouverture de crédit *f*

credit application form formule de crédit *f*

credit balance solde créditeur *m*, solde bénéficiaire *m*, solde actif *m*

credit bank banque de crédit *f*

credit card carte de crédit *f*

credit card insurance assurance des cartes de crédit *f*

credit card loan prêt sur carte de crédit *m*

credit card statement relevé des opérations de carte de crédit *m*

credit card transaction opération par carte de crédit *f*

credit ceiling plafond du crédit *m*

credit column colonne créditrice *f*

credit committee comité de crédit *m*

credit control [*by government*] encadrement du crédit *m*; [*by company*] contrôle de solvabilité *m*

credit controller contrôleur du crédit *m*

credit derivative dérivé de crédit *m*

credit-driven consumer spending consommation nourrie par le crédit *f*

credit enquiry renseignements de crédit *mpl*

credit exposure risque de crédit *m*

credit file dossier de crédit *m*

credit freeze gel de crédits *m*

credit institution établissement de crédit *m*, organisme de crédit *m*

credit instrument instrument de crédit *m*

credit interest intérêts créditeurs *mpl*

credit item poste créditeur *m*

credit limit limite de crédit *f*

credit management gestion de crédit *f*, direction des crédits *f*

credit manager responsable des engagements et des crédits *mf*

credit margin marge de crédit *f*

credit note note de crédit *f*, facture d'avoir *f*

credit officer spécialiste des crédits *mf*

credit period délai de paiement *m*

credit policy politique du crédit *f*

credit position position créditrice *f*

credit rating degré de solvabilité *m*, crédit scoring *m*

credit rating agency agence de notation *f*

credit restriction encadrement du crédit *m*

credit risk risque de crédit *m*, risque de signature *m*

credit scoring crédit scoring *m*, évaluation par score *f*

credit squeeze compression de crédit *f*, resserrement du crédit *m*

credit standing solvabilité *f*

credit union caisse de crédit mutuel *f*

credit-worthiness solvabilité *f*

credit-worthy solvable

credits [*item on statement*] crédit *m*

creditor créancier *m*

to **cross a cheque** barrer un chèque

cross-border transfrontière

cross-border payment paiement transfrontière *m*

cross-border trade opération transfrontière *f*

cross-currency swap crédit croisé *m*

cross-default clause clause de défaut croisé *f*

cross hedge couverture croisée *f*

cross trade application *f*, cross *m*

crossed cheque chèque barré *m*

cum div coupon attaché

cum dividend coupon attaché

cum rights droits attachés

cumulative balance solde cumulé *m*

cumulative credit crédit cumulé *m*

cumulative deficit déficit cumulé *m*

cumulative depreciation amortissements cumulés *mpl*

cumulative dividend dividende cumulatif *m*

currency devise *f*, monnaie *f*

currency advance avance en devises *f*

currency deposit dépôt en devise *m*

currency dealer cambiste *m*

currency derivative dérivé d'une monnaie *m*

currency fluctuation mouvement des devises *m*

currency futures contrats à terme sur devise *mpl*

currency market marché des devises *m*

currency option option sur devise *f*

currency swap échange de devises *m*, contrat de swap de devises *m*

currency transaction transaction en devises *f*

currency transfer transfert de devises *m*

current account compte chèque *m*, compte courant *m*

current assets actif circulant *m*

current liabilities passif circulant *m*, dettes à court terme *fpl*

current price cours instantané *m*

custodian conservateur *m*

custodian bank banque dépositaire *f*

custody garde *f*

customer client *m*; *customers* clientèle *f*

customer account compte client *m*

customer base clientèle *f*, base de clientèle *f*

customer code code client *m*

customer contact contact client *m*, contact clientèle *m*

customer credit crédit client *m*, avoir-client *m*

customer lending concours à la clientèle *m*

customer loans concours à la clientèle *m*

customer reference number code client *m*

customer relations manager directeur de la clientèle *m*

customer risk risque client *m*

customer service service à la clientèle *m*

D

D/A (= Documents against Acceptance) d/a

to **dabble on the stock market** boursicoter

dabbler on the stock market boursicoteur *m*

daily balance interest calculation méthode à échelles *f*, méthode par échelles *f*

daily rate cours du jour *m*

danger money prime de risque *f*

data analysis analyse des données *f*

data entry form fiche d'imputation *f*

data routing acheminement des données *m*

date-stamped record enregistrement horodaté *m*

dated security titre à échéance fixe *m*

dawn raid OPA inamicale *f*

DAX 30 index indice DAX 30 *m*

day before maturity veille de l'échéance *f*

day of grace jour de grâce *m*

day trade opération de journée *f*

daylight overdraft crédits intra-journaliers *mpl*

DD (= Direct Debit) prélèvement automatique *m*

deadline for payment date limite de paiement *f*

dealer négociateur *m*, marchand

de titres *m*

dealing négociation *f*

dealing room salle de marchés *f*

dealing room manager responsable de salle de marché *mf*

debenture, debenture bond obligation *f*

debenture *adj* obligataire

debit débit *m*; *to the debit of* au débit de

debit *adj* [*balance*] débiteur

to **debit** débiter; *to debit an account* débiter un compte; *to debit a sum to an account* débiter un compte d'une somme

debit account compte débiteur *m*

debit advice avis de débit *m*, avis de prélèvement *m*

debit and credit card law droit des cartes de paiement et de crédit *m*

debit balance solde débiteur *m*, solde passif *m*

debit card carte de débit *f*, carte de paiement *f*

debit column colonne débitrice *f*

debit interest intérêts débiteurs *mpl*

debit item poste débiteur *m*

debit note facture de débit *f*, facture de doit *f*, note de débit *f*

debit transfer transfert débiteur *m*

debits [*item on statement*] débit *m*

debits and credits doit et avoir *m*
debiting prélèvement *m*
debt dette *f*; [*to be recovered*] créance *f*; **to get into debt** s'endetter; **having dollar debts** endetté en dollars; **in debt** endetté
debt burden [*of country*] endettement *m*
debt chasing letter lettre de relance des impayés *f*
debt collection recouvrement de créances *m*
debt crisis crise de l'endettement *f*
debt-equity ratio ratio d'endettement *m*
debt equity swap échange de créances contre actifs *m*, conversion de créances en actions *f*
debt financing financement par endettement *m*, financement sur endettement *m*
debt-for-equity swap conversion de créances en actions *f*
debt instrument reconnaissance de dette *f*
debt management gestion des impayés *f*
debt not yet due créance non échue *f*
debt rescheduling rééchelonnement de dettes *m*
debt servicing service de la dette *m*
debt swap échange de créances *m*
debtor débiteur *m*
decentralization of capital décentralisation des capitaux *f*
to **decentralize** décentraliser; [*banks*] filialiser
decision support system système d'aide à la décision *m*

declaration of a dividend déclaration de dividende *f*
to **declare a dividend** déclarer un dividende
decrease décroissance *f*
to **deduct** déduire; [*sum*] décompter; [*at source, etc.*] prélever
to **deduct a commission** prélever une commission
to **deduct a sum of money** défalquer une somme
deduction at source retenue à la source *f*
deed acte *m*
deed of sale acte de vente *m*
deed of transfer acte de cession *m*
deep discount bond obligation très au-dessous du pair *f*
deep out of the money profondément hors des cours
default défaut de paiement *m*; [*of purchaser*] défaillance *f*
to **default** tomber en impayé
default interest intérêts moratoires *mpl*
default on payment défaut de paiement *m*
default rate taux de défaillance *m*
defaulter débiteur défaillant *m*
defaulting défaillant
to **defend a currency** défendre une devise
to **defer payment** différer le paiement
deferred debit débit différé *m*
deferred depreciation amortissements différés *mpl*
deferred future contrat à terme à échéance éloignée *m*
deflation déflation *f*
deficit déficit *m*; **to be in deficit** être en déficit

defrauder fraudeur *m*
to **delay payment** retarder le paiement
to **delist** radier de la cote, détacher à la cote
delisting radiation de la cote *f*, détachement à la cote *m*
to **deliver** livrer
to **deliver shares** délivrer des valeurs
delivery livraison *f*
delivery month mois de livraison *m*
delivery of securities livraison des titres *f*, délivrance de titres *f*
delivery procedure procédure de livraison *f*
delta delta
demand: on demand sur demande, sur requête
to **demand payment** réclamer le paiement
demand deposit remise à vue *f*, dépôt à vue *m*
demand deposit account compte à vue *m*
demand-led tiré par la demande
demand-pull inflation inflation par la demande *f*
dematerialization dématérialisation *f*
to **demonetize** démonétiser
demonetization démonétisation *f*
to **denominate** libeller
denominated in dollars libellé en dollars
denomination coupure *f*
departmental manager chef de service *m*
depersonalization dépersonnalisation *f*
deposit dépôt *m*
to **deposit** déposer

to **deposit a sum of money** consigner une somme
to **deposit shares as security** nantir des valeurs
to **deposit sth as security** gager qch
deposit account compte de dépôt *m*, compte d'épargne *m*
deposit at call dépôt à vue *m*
deposit bank banque de dépôt *f*
deposit money monnaie scripturale *f*
deposit protection scheme système de protection des dépôts *m*
deposit protection fund fonds de protection des dépôts *m*
deposit-taking institution établissement collecteur de dépôts *m*
depositary dépositaire *m*
depositor déposant *m*
to **depreciate** se déprécier
depreciated amorti
depreciation dépréciation *f*
deputy manager (of a branch) sous-directeur (d'une succursale) *m*
to **deregulate** déréglementer
deregulation déréglementation *f*, décloisonnement *m*
deregulation of the banking system déréglementation bancaire *f*
derivative produit dérivé *m*
derivatives dealer négociateur en produits dérivés *m*
to **destabilize** déstabiliser
destabilizing déstabilisateur
devaluation dévaluation *f*
to **devalue** dévaluer
development capital capital-développement *m*

development loans crédits de développement *mpl*

diagonal spread écart diagonal *m*, spread diagonal *m*

difference in prices différence de cours *f*

difference in the rate différence de cours *f*

direct banking banque à distance *f*

direct debit prélèvement automatique *m*

direct debit advice avis de prélèvement automatique *m*

direct debit mandate ordre de prélèvement *m*, autorisation de prélèvement *f*

direct financing finance directe *f*, financement direct *m*

direct shareholder détenteur direct d'actions *m*

disbursement déboursement *m*, décaissement *m*

discharge of a debt extinction d'une dette *f*

to **discharge a debt** apurer une dette

to **discharge a debtor** libérer un débiteur

to **discharge sb from a debt** décharger qn d'une dette

discharged bankrupt failli réhabilité *m*

disclosure threshold seuil d'annonce obligatoire *m*

discount [*on Stock Exchange*] décote *f*; [*of debts*] escompte *m*; [*commercial*] remise *f*

to **discount** escompter

discount broker courtier exécutant *m*

discount house comptoir d'escompte *m*

discount rate taux d'escompte *m*;

[*for calculating NPV*] taux d'actualisation *m*

discountable escomptable

discounted bill effet escompté *m*

discretionary account compte sous mandat de gestion *m*

discretionary limit [*of bank manager*] plafond autorisé *m*

discretionary management mandat général d'administration *m*

discretionary order ordre environ *m*

dishonoured bill effet en souffrance *m*

disinflation désinflation *f*

to **disintermediate** désintermédier

disintermediation désintermédiation *f*

disparity décalage *m*

dispensing machine distributeur automatique *m*

distribution network réseau de distribution *m*

distribution of profit distribution d'un bénéfice *f*

diversified diversifié

to **divest** désinvestir des capitaux

divestment désinvestissement *m*

dividend dividende *m*

dividend announcement déclaration de dividende *f*

dividend share action de jouissance *f*

divisional account compte divisionnaire *m*

documentary bill traite documentaire *f*

documentary credit crédit documentaire *m*, crédoc *m*

documentary letter of credit lettre de crédit documentaire *f*

documents against acceptance
documents contre acceptation
documents against payment
documents contre paiement
dollar account compte en
dollar *m*
dollar area zone dollar *f*
domestic market marché
domestique *m*
domestic transaction opération
domestique *f*
domicile domicile *m*
to **domicile** domicilier
domiciliation domiciliation *f*
dormant account compte sans
mouvement *m*
double charging double
tarification *f*
double option stellage *m*
doubtful debt client douteux *m*
doubtful debt provisions réserves
pour créances douteuses *fpl*
doubtful debtor client douteux *m*
Dow Jones index indice Dow
Jones *m*
down: to be down by [*of prices,
rates, etc.*] être en baisse de
down payment acompte *m*
downside risk risque de baisse *m*
downturn in the market
retournement de marché *m*
downward effect effet
réducteur *m*

downward movement mouvement
de baisse *m*
downward trend tendance à la
baisse *f*
**D/P (= Documents against
Payment)** d/p
draft effet *m*; [*bill of exchange*]
traite *f*
draw tirer
to **draw a bill on** tirer une traite sur
to **draw a cheque on** tirer un
chèque sur, disposer un chèque
sur
to **draw at sight** tirer à vue
to **draw cash** retirer des espèces
drawdown tirage *m*
drawee tiré *m*
drawee's risk risque tiré *m*
drawer tireur *m*; [*of commercial
bill*] souscripteur *m*
drawing [*for bonds to be
redeemed*] tirage au sort *m*
drawing rights droits de
tirage *mpl*
to **drop** [*market prices*] reculer
dud cheque chèque en bois *m*
due dû; *to become due on ...*
arriver à échéance le ...
due date date d'échéance *f*, date
d'exigibilité *f*
duty of vigilance devoir de
vigilance *m*

E

early exercise exercice
prématuré *m*

early exit risk risque de sortie
anticipée *m*

early redemption remboursement
anticipé *m*, amortissement
anticipé *m*

early repayment remboursement
anticipé *m*

early warning system gestion
d'alertes *f*

to **earn money** gagner de l'argent

earnings per share bénéfice par
action *m*

to **ease** fléchir

easily realizable assets actifs
facilement mobilisables *mpl*

to **eat a card** [*of cash machine*]
avaler une carte

**EBDIT (= Earnings Before
Depreciation, Interest and
Tax)** EBE *m*

**EBF (= European Banking
Federation)** Fbe *f*

**EBRD (= European Bank for
Reconstruction and
Development)** BERD *f*

e-cash monnaie électronique *f*

**Echo (= European Clearing
Houses Organization)** Echo *m*

econometric économétrique

Economic and Monetary Union
Union économique et
monétaire *f*

economic growth croissance
économique *f*

economic indicator indicateur
économique *m*, clignotant
économique *m*

**ECU (= European Currency
Unit)** écu *m*

**EFTPOS (= Electronic Funds
Transfer at the Point-Of-Sale)**
transfert de fonds électronique à
partir du point de vente *m*

**EFTS (= Electronic Funds
Transfer System)** système de
transfert de fonds
électronique *m*

**EIB (= European Investment
Bank)** BEI *f*

electronic banking bancatique *f*,
banque électronique *f*

electronic cash monnaie
électronique *f*

electronic clearing compensation
électronique *f*

electronic currency monnaie
électronique *f*

electronic data interchange
échange de données informatisé
m, EDI *m*

electronic data processing
informatique *f*

electronic data transmission
télématique *f*

electronic funds transfer transfert
électronique de fonds *m*

electronic funds transfer at the point-of-sale transfert de fonds électronique à partir du point de vente *m*

electronic funds transfer system système de transfert de fonds électronique *m*

electronic invoice facture électronique *f*

electronic invoice management gestion électronique de factures *f*

electronic mail messagerie *f*, courrier électronique *m*

electronic money monnaie électronique *f*

electronic payment paiement électronique *m*

electronic payment system système électronique de paiement *m*

electronic payment terminal terminal électronique de paiement *m*

electronic purse porte-monnaie électronique *m*

electronic terminal terminal électronique *m*

electronic transactions masse électronique *f*

electronic transfer filière électronique *f*

electronic wallet porte-monnaie électronique *m*

eligible bank banque éligible *f*

eligible banker's acceptance acceptance de banquier éligible au réescompte *f*

to embezzle money détourner de l'argent

e-money monnaie électronique *f*

employee share ownership scheme plan d'épargne d'entreprise *m*, PEE *m*

EMS (= European Monetary System) SME *m*

EMU (= Economic and Monetary Union) UEM *f*

to encumber grever

encumbered grevé

end-of-month payments échéances de fin de mois *fpl*

end-of-month settlement liquidation de fin de mois *f*

end-of-month statement relevé de fin de mois *m*

end of the financial year clôture de l'exercice *f*, fin de l'exercice *f*

endorsable endossable

to endorse endosser

endorsed bill effet endossé *m*

endorsee endossataire *mf*

endorsement endos *m*, endossement *m*

endorsement commission commission d'endos *f*

endorsement fee commission d'endos *f*

endorser endosseur *m*

endowment mortgage crédit immobilier garanti par une assurance-vie *m*

endowment policy assurance-vie (remboursable à terme fixe ou à la mort du titulaire) *f*

to enter into commitments contracter des engagements

entitlement to interest jouissance d'intérêts *f*

equalization payment soulte *f*

equity fonds propres *mpl*

equity-based à base d'actions

equity(-based) derivative dérivé d'actions *m*

equity-based unit trust sicav actions *f*

equity capital capitaux propres *mpl*

equity investment titre de participation *m*

equity-linked debt titres assimilés à des actions *mpl*

equity loan titre participatif *m*, prêt participatif *m*

equity market marché des actions *m*, marché des valeurs *m*

equity trader négociateur en actions *m*, négociateur en valeurs *m*

equity trading négociation en actions *f*, négociation en valeurs *f*

equity unit trust sicav actions *f*

ERM (= Exchange Rate Mechanism) mécanisme de change *m*

erosion érosion *f*

erosion of prices effritement des cours *m*

escrow blocage *m*; *in escrow* bloqué

escrow account compte bloqué *m*

escrow current account compte courant bloqué *m*

estimate devis *m*

Eurobank eurobanque *f*

Eurobond euro-obligation *f*

Eurobond market marché euro-obligataire *m*

Eurocard Eurocard

Eurocheque eurochèque *m*

Eurocommercial paper effets de commerce en eurodevises *mpl*

Eurocurrency eurodevise *f*

Eurodollar eurodollar *m*

Eurodollar future contrat à terme sur l'eurodollar *m*

Eurofranc eurofranc *m*

Euro-issue euro-émission *f*

Euroloan eurocrédit *m*, euro-emprunt *m*, crédit en euro-devises *m*

Euromarket marché de l'Eurodevise *m*, marché financier européen *m*

Euronote euro-billet *m*

Europay Europay

European Banking Standards Committee Comité Européen de Normalisation Bancaire *m*

European central bank banque centrale européenne *f*

European currency unit écu *m*

European exchange rate mechanism mécanisme de change européen *m*

European financial market marché financier européen *m*

European Investment Bank Banque européenne d'investissement *f*

European Monetary Institute Institut monétaire européen *m*

European Monetary System Système monétaire européen *m*

European Monetary Union Union Européenne Monétaire *f*

European(-style) option option européenne *f*

to **even out** s'équilibrer

event of default déchéance du terme *f*

to **exceed** dépasser

to **exceed a credit limit** dépasser un crédit

to **exceed a threshold** dépasser un seuil

excess cover sur-couverture *f*

excess margin excédent de dépôt de garantie *m*

excessive taxation fiscalité excessive *f*

exchange adjustments écarts de conversion *mpl*

exchange commission commission de change *f*

exchange control regulations réglementation du change *f*

exchange control system système de contrôle des changes *m*

exchange controls contrôle des changes *m*

exchange gain gain de change *m*

exchange of goods échange de marchandises *m*

exchange price prix boursier *m*

exchange rate taux du change *m*

exchange rate fluctuation fluctuation des cours *f*

exchange rate gain gain de change *m*

exchange rate loss perte de change *f*

exchange rate mechanism mécanisme de change *m*

exchange rate parity parités du change *fpl*

exchange rate stability stabilité des changes *f*

exchange rate swap swap de change *m*

exchange rates cours des changes *m*

Exchequer *Br* ministère des Finances *m*

ex-coupon coupon détaché

ex-div coupon détaché, coupon échu

ex-dividend coupon détaché, coupon échu

execution [*of an order*] exécution *f*

execution at market exécution au prix du marché *f*

exemption exonération *f*

exercisable exerçable

exercise [*of an option*] exercice *m*

to **exercise an option** exercer une option

to **exercise an option at maturity** exercer (une option) à l'échéance

to **exercise at maturity** exercer à l'échéance

to **exercise in advance** exercer par anticipation

exercise cut-off time délai limite de levée *m*

exercise date date d'exercice *f*

exercise instruction instruction d'exercice *f*

exercise limit limite à l'exercice *f*

exercise notice avis de levée *m*, avis d'exercice *m*

exercise price prix de levée *m*, prix d'exercice *m*

expectation: in the expectation of en prévision de

expected financial flow flux financier anticipé *m*

expenditure dépenses *fpl*

expiration series série d'échéances *f*

to **expire** expirer

expiry expiration *f*; *before expiry* avant l'échéance

expiry date date d'échéance *f*, date d'expiration *f*

expiry month mois d'expiration *m*

export exportation *f*

export credit crédit à l'exportation *m*

export finance financement des exportations *m*

export financing financement des exportations *m*

export lending concours à l'exportation *m*

export loans concours à l'exportation *m*

exposure engagement *m*, exposition aux risques *f*, risque *m*

to **expropriate** exproprier

expropriation expropriation *f*

ex-rights droit détaché

to **extend a loan** [*grant*] octroyer un crédit; [*prolong*] prolonger un crédit

to **extend payment terms** proroger une échéance

extent of a loss étendue d'une perte *f*

external financing financement extérieur *m*

extra time to pay sursis de paiement *m*

face [*of bill*] recto *m*

face value valeur faciale *f*, taux facial *m*

facility fee [*for overdraft*] commission de confirmation *f*

factoring affacturage *m*

factoring company société d'affacturage *f*

fair market value valeur vénale *f*

fair value [*of an option*] valeur juste *f*

to **fall** [*shares, rates*] s'inscrire en baisse

to **fall back** [*currency*] déprécier

to **fall due** échoir, arriver à échéance

to **fall in value** se déclasser

fall in prices fléchissement des prix *m*, chute des cours *f*

fall in share prices tassement des actions *m*

falling [*market*] orienté à la baisse

fan club club des amis *m*

Fannie Mae *Am* fonds fédéral de refinancement de créances hypothécaires *m*; [*certificate*] créance hypothécaire *f*

far month échéance éloignée *f*

favour: in favour of en faveur de

fax fax *m*

Fed *Am* Fed *f*

Fed funds *Am* fonds fédéraux *mpl*

Fed funds rate *Am* taux de fonds fédéraux *m*

Federal funds *Am* fonds fédéraux *mpl*

Federal funds market *Am* marché de fonds fédéraux *m*

Federal Home Loan Mortgage

Corporation *Am* organisme de titrisation des créances hypothécaires *m*

Federal National Mortgage Association *Am* fonds fédéral de refinancement de créances hypothécaires *m*

Federal Reserve *Am* réserve fédérale *f*

Federal reserve bank *Am* banque de réserve fédérale *f*

Federal Reserve System *Am* "Fed" *f*

fee commission *f*

fee note note de commission *f*

fiat money monnaie fiduciaire *f*, monnaie à cours forcé *f*

fictitious asset actif fictif *m*

fiduciary account compte fiduciaire *m*

fiduciary duty devoir fiduciaire *m*

figure chiffre *m*; *in figures* en chiffres

file [*paper, computer*] fichier *m*; [*paper*] dossier *m*

to **file for bankruptcy** déposer son bilan

filing for bankruptcy dépôt de bilan *m*

fill or kill order ordre exécution immédiate ou annulation *m*

final balance solde de tout compte *m*, résultat final *m*

final discharge quittance finale *f*

final dividend dividende définitif *m*, dividende final *m*

final payment quittance finale *f*

finance finance *f*

to **finance** financer

finance act loi des finances *f*

finance company société financière *f*

finance house société financière *f*

finance lease location-financement *m*

financed from cashflow autofinancé

financial financier

financial accounting comptabilité générale *f*

financial adviser conseiller financier *m*

financial aid aide financière *f*

financial asset actif financier *m*

financial attribute attribut financier *m*

financial bubble bulle financière *f*

financial centre place financière *f*

financial circles sphères de la finance *fpl*

financial circulation circuit financier *m*, circuits financiers *mpl*

financial consultant conseiller financier *m*

financial controller contrôleur financier *m*

financial costs frais financiers *mpl*

financial data données financières *fpl*

financial debt dette financière *f*

financial deregulation déréglementation financière *f*

financial division division financière *f*

financial expert expert financier *m*

financial field domaine financier *m*

financial firm cabinet financier *m*

financial future instrument financier à terme *m*

financial health check diagnostic financier *m*

financial institution établissement financier *m*, organisme financier *m*

financial instrument instrument financier *m*

financial integration intégration financière *f*

financial intermediary intermédiaire financier *m*

financial investment placement financier *m*

financial legislation législation financière *f*

financial leverage levier financier *m*

financial management gestion financière *f*, direction financière *f*

financial management accounting comptabilité-gestion financière *f*

financial management ratio ratio de gestion financière *m*

financial market marché financier *m*

financial marketing marketing financier *m*

financial marketplace place financière *f*

financial means moyens financiers *mpl*

financial newspaper journal financier *m*

financial package montage financier *m*

financial plan plan de financement *m*

financial position position financière *f*

financial press presse financière *f*

financial ratio ratio de situation *m*, ratio de gestion financière *m*

financial resources ressources financières *fpl*

financial services services financiers *mpl*

financial services company société de services financiers *f*

financial services industry secteur des services financiers *m*

financial situation situation financière *f*

financial standing solvabilité *f*

financial statement état financier *m*, bilan financier *m*

financial syndicate syndicat financier *m*

financial transaction opération financière *f*

financial year exercice *m*, année fiscale *f*

financially financièrement

financier financier *m*

financing financement *m*

financing capacity capacité de financement *f*

financing from cashflow autofinancement *m*

financing mechanism mécanisme de financement *m*

financing product produit de financement *m*

financing structure structure de financement *f*

firm of brokers maison de courtage *f*

firm of financial experts cabinet d'experts financiers *m*

firm option option ferme *f*

firm order ordre ferme *m*

firm price prix ferme *m*

firm sale vente ferme *f*

firm transactions opérations fermes *fpl*

firmness of the market fermeté des cours *f*

first legal mortgage hypothèque de premier rang *f*

first of exchange première de change *f*

first quarter premier trimestre *m*

fiscal fiscal

fiscal year *Am* exercice *m*, exercice budgétaire *m*, année budgétaire *f*, année fiscale *f*

to **fix a price** fixer un prix

fixed fixe

fixed annual payment annuité constante *f*

fixed asset actif immobilisé *m*, immobilisation *f*

fixed capital capital fixe *m*

fixed-date bill effet à date fixe *m*

fixed income asset actif de taux *m*

fixed income investment placement à revenus fixes *m*

fixed income security titre à revenu fixe *m*, valeur à revenu fixe *f*

fixed interest intérêt fixe *m*

fixed interest security valeur à revenu fixe *f*

fixed maturity date échéance contractuelle *f*

fixed parity area zone de parités fixes *f*

fixed rate taux fixe *m*, TF *m*

fixed-rate à taux fixe

fixed-rate bond obligation à revenu fixe *f*

fixed-rate mortgage (loan) crédit hypothécaire à taux fixe *m*

fixed-rate of interest taux d'intérêt fixe *m*

fixed-term credit crédit à durée déterminée *m*

fixing of quotas (on) contingentement (de) *m*

flat rate taux uniforme *m*, taux forfaitaire *m*

flight of capital fuite de capitaux *f*, évasion de capitaux *f*

float float *m*, flottant *m*

to **float** faire flotter

floating assets actif circulant *m*

floating capital capital flottant *m*

floating charge nantissement "flottant" *m*, nantissement général *m*

floating rate bond obligation à revenu variable *f*

floating rate CD CD à taux flottant *m*

floating rate certificate of deposit certificat de dépôt à taux flottant *m*

floating rate loan crédit à taux variable *m*

floating rate note effet à taux flottant *m*, effet à taux révisable *m*

floating rate of exchange taux de change flottant *m*

floating rate of interest taux d'intérêt flottant *m*

floating rate security titre à revenu variable *m*, valeur à revenu variable *f*

floor [*of Stock Exchange*] parquet *m*; [*of rate*] plancher *m*, taux plancher *m*

flotation émission d'actions en Bourse *f*; [*of company*] introduction en Bourse *f*

flow of finance flux financier *m*

flow of funds flux des fonds *m*

to **fluctuate** fluctuer, osciller

fluctuation fluctuation *f*, oscillation *f*

Footsie (= Financial Times Stock Exchange) ≈ CAC 40 *m*

to **forecast a fall** prévoir une baisse

forecast balance sheet bilan de prévoyance *m*

to **foreclose on a loan** interrompre un crédit, rompre un crédit avant son terme

foreclosure forclusion *f*

foreign bank banque étrangère *f*

foreign bond obligation étrangère *f*

foreign currency devise étrangère *f*, devises étrangères *fpl*

foreign currency account compte en devises étrangères *m*

foreign currency assets avoirs en devises étrangères *mpl*

foreign currency cheque chèque en devise *m*

foreign currency credit crédit en devise *m*

foreign currency holding avoir en devises *m*

foreign currency option option de change *f*

foreign currency payment paiement en devise *m*

foreign currency reserves réserves en devises *fpl*

foreign exchange change *m*

foreign exchange broker cambiste *mf*

foreign exchange controls contrôle des changes *m*

foreign exchange counter bureau de change *m*

foreign exchange department service du change *m*

foreign exchange dealer cambiste *mf*

foreign exchange exposure risque de (taux de) change *m*

foreign exchange gain gain de change *m*

foreign exchange loss perte de change *f*

foreign exchange market marché des changes *m*

foreign exchange risk risque de change *m*

foreign exchange services services de change *mpl*

foreign exchange trade opération de change *f*

foreign investor investisseur étranger *m*

foreign securities valeurs étrangères *fpl*

foreign security exchange currency devise-titre *f*

forex (= FORreign EXchange)

forfait: à forfait à forfait

forfaiting forfaitage *m*, forfaitisation *f*

forfeit dédit *m*

forged [*banknote*] faux

forged cheque faux chèque *m*

forgery falsification *f*

form imprimé *m*

formal notice mise en demeure *f*

fortnightly settlement liquidation de quinzaine *f*

forward à terme

forward account compte à terme *m*

forward contract contrat de couverture à terme *m*

forward exchange change à terme *m*

forward price cours à terme *m*

forward purchase achat à terme *m*

forward quotation cotation à terme *f*

forward rate agreement accord de taux futur *m*

FRA (= Forward Rate Agreement) ATF *m*

fraction fraction *f*

fractional rights rompus *mpl*

franc franc *m*

franc-mark parity parité franc-mark *f*

fraud fraude *f*

fraudulent frauduleux

fraudulent usage [*of credit card*] utilisation frauduleuse *f*

fraudulently frauduleusement

FRCD (= Floating Rate Certificate of Deposit) CD à taux flottant *m*

Freddie Mac *Am* organisme de titrisation des créances hypothécaires *m;* [*certificate*] créance hypothécaire *f*

free [*no charge*] gratuit; *to be free of a debt* être quitte d'une dette

free banking banque sans frais de compte *f*

freefall chute ample *f*

free movement of capital libre circulation des capitaux *f*

free reserves *Am* réserves disponibles *fpl*

to **freeze** bloquer

friendly takeover bid OPA amicale *f*

FRN (= Floating-Rate Note) effet à taux révisable *m*

front-end costs, front-load fees [*for fund*] frais d'entrée *mpl*

front office salle des guichets *f*,

front-office *m*

frozen gelé

frozen credit crédit bloqué *m*

FT 100 index indice FT 100 *m*

full-service bank banque universelle *f*

fully paid-up intégralement libéré

fully paid-up securities titres libérés *mpl*

to **fund** financer

fund management gestion de fonds *f*, gestion de capitaux *f*

fund manager gérant de portefeuille *m*, dirigeant d'OPCVM *m*

fund transfer transfert de fonds *m*

funded pension scheme contrat de retraite par capitalisation *m*

funding financement *m*, provisionnement *m*

funding method méthode de financement *f*

funding plan plan de financement *m*

funds: in funds [*account*] provisionné

fungible fongible

future contrat à terme *m*

futures contract contrat à terme *m*

futures exchange marché à terme *m*

futures market marché à terme *m*

futures order ordre à terme *m*

futures trading négociations à terme *fpl*

fx (= Foreign Exchange)

121

G

gain plus-value *f*

to **gain against the dollar** apprécier contre le dollar

gain in value plus-value *f*

gamma gamma *m*

gap gap *m*

garnishee order saisie-arrêt *f*

GDP (= Gross Domestic Product) PIB *m*

gearing endettement *m*

general mortgage hypothèque générale *f*

general provisions fonds pour risques bancaires généraux *m*

generalized bank banque généraliste *f*

gilt-edged stock valeurs de père de famille *fpl*

gilts *Br* valeurs de père de famille *fpl*; [*government stock*] obligations du Trésor *fpl*

Ginnie Mae *Am* fonds public de refinancement de créances hypothécaires *m*; [*certificate*] créance hypothécaire *f*

giro account compte chèque postal *m*, compte courant postal *m*, CCP *m*

Girobank banque postale *f*

giro transfer transfert par CCP *m*

global banking banque universelle *f*

global custody service [*for fund managers*] service de conservation des titres *m*

global outlay débours global *m*

global position position globale *f*

globalization [*generalization*] globalisation *f*; [*making worldwide*] mondialisation *f*

to **globalize** [*generalize*] globaliser; [*make worldwide*] mondialiser

globally globalement; [*worldwide*] mondialement

GNP (= Gross National Product) PNB *m*

gold or *m*

gold assets avoirs en or *mpl*

gold bullion or en barres *m*, or en lingots *m*

gold card carte privilégiée *f*

gold clause clause or *f*

gold standard étalon or *m*

gold value of the franc franc or *m*

golden share action spécifique *f*

good investment placement avantageux *m*

good-till-cancelled order ordre à révocation *m*

government bond obligation d'État *f*, titre de rente *m*

Government funds fonds de l'État *mpl*, fonds publics *mpl*

Government National Mortgage Association *Am* fonds public de refinancement de créances hypothécaires *m*

Governor of the Bank of England Gouverneur de la Banque d'Angleterre *m*

grand total total général *m*

granny bond bon d'épargne réservé aux personnes âgées *m*

to **grant** accorder

to **grant a loan** octroyer un prêt, ouvrir un crédit

granter of an option optionnaire *mf*

granting octroi *m*

granting of a loan octroi d'un prêt *m*, ouverture de crédit *f*

greenback billet vert *m*, dollar américain *m*

greenmail greenmail *m*

grey market marché gris *m*

gross montant brut *m*

gross *adj* brut

gross amount montant brut *m*

gross dividend dividende brut *m*

gross domestic product produit intérieur brut *m*

gross interest intérêts bruts *mpl*

gross loss perte brute *f*

gross national product produit national brut *m*

gross operating profit résultat brut d'exploitation *m*

gross rate taux brut *m*

gross revenue recettes brutes *fpl*

gross settlement règlement brut *m*

gross yield to redemption rémunération brute actuarielle *f*

growth croissance *f*

growth rate rythme de croissance *m*

growth stock action de croissance *f*

guarantee garantie *f*; [*surety, security*] cautionnement *m*, caution *f*

to **guarantee** garantir; [*with surety*] cautionner

to **guarantee sb's creditworthiness** garantir la solvabilité de qn

guarantee commission commission de garantie *f*

guaranteed bond obligation garantie *f*

guaranteed growth bond bon de capitalisation *m*

guaranteed income instrument produit garanti *m*

guaranteed investment produit garanti *m*

guaranteed yield rendement garanti *m*

guarantor garant *m*; [*of bill of exchange*] avaliste *m*, donneur d'aval *m*

H

half-monthly settlement liquidation de quinzaine *f*
half-yearly semestriel
to **handle money** manier de l'argent
handling charge frais d'administration *mpl*
hard currency devise forte *f*
head office siège social *m*
hedge couverture *f*
to **hedge** *vt* couvrir
to **hedge** *vi* se couvrir
to **hedge against** se couvrir contre
to **hedge a position** couvrir une position, protéger une position
to **hedge a risk** couvrir un risque
hedge ratio ratio de couverture *m*
hedger opérateur en couverture *m*
hedging couverture *f*, couverture de risques *f*
hedging instrument outil de couverture *m*
hedging market marché de couverture *m*
hedging of a position protection d'une position *f*
hedging of exchange rate risks couverture de changes *f*
hedging strategy stratégie de couverture *f*
hidden costs coûts cachés *mpl*
high and low prices cours extrêmes *mpl*

high street bank *Br* banque populaire *f*, banque à réseau *f*
to **hit a bid** accepter un cours acheteur
to **hold a lease on** tenir à bail
to **hold as security** détenir en garantie
to **hold shares** détenir des actions; *to hold 5% of the shares in* détenir 5% du capital de
to **hold steady** se maintenir
holder détenteur *m*, titulaire *mf*
holder in due course tiers porteur *m*
holder of an option détenteur d'une option *m*
holding [*of shares, options, etc.*] détention *f*; [*shareholding*] participation *f*
holding company holding *m*, société holding *f*
hole-in-the-wall machine point argent *m*
home banking banque à domicile *f*
home insurance assurance habitation *f*
home loan crédit immobilier *m*, prêt à l'habitat *m*
home loans crédit à l'habitat *m*
home purchase loan crédit épargne-logement *m*
honest accounting enregistrement comptable sincère *m*

horizon of expectation horizon d'anticipation *m*
horizontal spread écart horizontal *m*, spread horizontal *m*
hostile takeover bid OPA inamicale *f*
hot money capitaux fébriles *mpl*
hour: *before hours* avant Bourse;

after hours après Bourse
household consumer spending consommation des ménages *f*
household saving épargne des ménages *f*
hundred centaine *f*
hybrid hybride
hybrid rate taux hybride *m*

I

IBOR (= InterBank Offered Rate) TIO *m*
IBRD (= International Bank for Reconstruction and Development) BIRD *f*
IDA (=International Development Association) AID *f*
idle [*capital*] oisif, improductif
illiquid illiquide, peu liquide
IMF (= International Monetary Fund) FMI *m*
immediate debit débit immédiat *m*
immediate or cancel order ordre exécution immédiate ou annulation *m*
immediately due exigibilité immédiate
impact: *to have an impact on price* avoir une incidence sur le cours

implied volatility volatilité implicite *f*
import importation *f*
imprinter facturette *f*
improved cashflow trésorerie aisée *f*
income revenu *m*; [*from investment, shares*] rente *f*
income for life rente viagère *f*
income stock actions à fort rendement *fpl*
to **increase a position** accroître une position
increase in bank lending gonflement du volume du crédit *m*
increase in capital augmentation de capital *f*
increase in revenues augmentation des revenus *f*
increase in value plus-value *f*

125

to **incur a loss** [*person*] subir une perte financière; [*deal*] entraîner une perte

to **incur costs** encourir des frais

to **incur debts** contracter des dettes

indebtedness endettement *m*

indemnification dédommagement *m*

index indice *m*

index-based indiciel

index-linked indexé

index-linked bond obligation indexée *f*

index-linking indexation *f*

index option option sur indice *f*

indexation indexation *f*

indexed loan emprunt indexé *m*

industrials valeurs des sociétés industrielles *fpl*

inflation inflation *f*

inflation rate taux d'inflation *m*

inflationary inflationniste

initial capital capital initial *m*

initial margin dépôt de garantie *m*

initial price cours initial *m*

insider dealing délit d'initié *m*

insider trading délit d'initié *m*

insolvency insolvabilité *f*

insolvent insolvable

instalment tranche de paiement *f*, versement (partiel) *m*

instalment credit crédit remboursable par acomptes *m*

instalment payment règlement à crédit *m*

instant access account compte d'épargne à retrait immédiat *m*

instant(aneous) settlement règlement instantané *m*

instant balance solde instantané *m*

institutional investors investisseurs institutionnels *mpl*, zinzins *mpl*

instrument titre *m*

instrument to order papier à ordre *m*

insufficient funds provision insuffisante *f*, insuffisance de provision *f*

insurance adviser conseiller assurances *m*

insurance banker bancassureur *m*

insurance code code des assurances *m*

insurance commission commission d'assurance *f*

insurance company compagnie d'assurance *f*

insurance consultant conseiller assurances *m*

insurance derivative dérivé d'assurance *m*

insurance policy police d'assurance *f*

insurance-related savings products assurfinance *f*

insurer assureur *m*

intangible asset actif incorporel *m*, immobilisation incorporelle *f*

interbank interbancaire

interbank clearing system système de compensation interbancaire *m*

interbank competition compétition interbancaire *f*

interbank computerized clearing system système interbancaire de télécompensation *m*

interbank deposit dépôt interbancaire *m*

interbank loan prêt interbancaire *m*

interbank market marché interbancaire *m*

interbank money argent de gré à gré entre banques *m*

interbank offered rate taux interbanque offert *m*

interbank rate taux interbancaire *m*

interbank trading échange interbancaire *m*

interbank transfer virement interbancaire *m*

intercompany interentreprise

interconnection interconnexion *f*

inter-dealer trading négociation entre courtiers *f*

interest intérêt *m*; *to bear/carry/ yield interest* porter/produire/ rapporter des intérêts

interest accrued intérêts courus *mpl*, fraction d'intérêt *f*

interest and other finance charges charges financières *fpl*

interest-bearing [*investment*] rémunérateur, productif d'intérêts

interest-bearing account compte rémunéré *m*

interest-bearing investments investissements productifs *mpl*

interest charge charge d'intérêt *f*

interest days jours d'intérêt *mpl*

interest due intérêts dus *mpl*, intérêts exigibles *mpl*

interest due and payable intérêts exigibles *mpl*

interest-free loan prêt sans intérêt *m*

interest income produits financiers *mpl*

interest margin marge d'intérêt *f*; [*earned by a bank*] marge d'intermédiation *f*

interest on arrears intérêt de retard *m*

interest on capital rémunération de capital *f*

interest on late payment intérêt de retard *m*

interest paid intérêt servi *m*, intérêts versés *mpl*

interest rate taux d'intérêt *m*

interest rate arbitrage arbitrage des taux d'intérêt *m*

interest rate ceiling plafond des taux d'intérêt *m*

interest rate differential différentiel de taux d'intérêt *m*

interest rate fluctuations fluctuations de taux d'intérêt *fpl*

interest rate future contrat à terme sur taux d'intérêts *m*

interest rate mismatch transformation des taux d'intérêt *f*

interest rate option option de taux d'intérêt *f*

interest rate period période de validité d'un taux d'intérêt *f*

interest rate risk risque de taux d'intérêt *m*, aléa des taux d'intérêt *m*

interest rate spread marge sur taux *f*

interest rate swap contrat de swap de taux d'intérêt *m*, échange de taux d'intérêt *m*

interest received intérêts perçus *mpl*

interim dividend dividende intérimaire *m*, dividende intermédiaire *m*, acompte sur dividende *m*

interim statement bilan intérimaire *m*

intermediate broker remisier *m*

127

intermediated intermédié

intermediation intermédiation *f*

internal audit audit interne *m*

internal auditing contrôle interne *m*

internal auditor réviseur interne *m*

internal rate of return taux interne de rentabilité *m*

international banking banque internationale *f*

international banking syndicate syndicat bancaire international *m*

international currency monnaie internationale *f*

International Bank for Reconstruction and Development Banque internationale pour la reconstruction et le développement *f*

International Development Association Association internationale de développement *f*

international exchange Bourse internationale *f*

international liquid assets liquidités internationales *fpl*

International Monetary Fund Fonds monétaire international *m*

international monetary system système monétaire international *m*

international payment paiement international *m*

interoperability interopérabilité *f*

interoperable interopérable

inter-system standard norme intersystème *f*

intervention rate taux d'intervention *m*

intrinsic value valeur intrinsèque *f*

introduction on the Stock Exchange introduction en Bourse *f*; [*of shares*] émission en Bourse *f*

to **invest** investir

to **invest short-term** placer à court terme

investment investissement *m*, placement *m*

investment advice conseil financier *m*; [*for personal assets*] conseil patrimonial *m*

investment adviser conseiller en placement *m*; [*for personal assets*] conseiller patrimonial *m*

investment bank [*in the US*] banque d'affaires *f*

investment banker banquier d'affaires *m*

investment banking banque d'affaires *f*, banque d'investissement *f*

investment capital capital-investissement *m*

investment capital company société de capital-investissement *f*

investment company société d'investissement *f*

investment consultancy conseil en investissement *m*; [*for personal assets*] conseil patrimonial *m*

investment consultant conseiller en placement *m*; [*for personal assets*] conseiller patrimonial *m*

investment consultants société de conseil en investissement *f*

investment credit crédit d'investissement *m*

investment fund fonds d'investissement *m*, organisme de placement collectif *m*

investment manager gestionnaire de placement *mf*
investment rate taux de placement *m*
investment regulations règles de placement *fpl*
investment trust fonds commun de placement *m*, FCP *m*
investor investisseur *m*
invoice facture *f*
invoicing facturation *f*
to **invoke a guarantee** faire jouer une garantie
irredeemable [*bond*] irrachetable, irremboursable
irrevocability irrévocabilité *f*
irrevocable irrévocable
irrevocable letter of credit lettre de crédit irrévocable *f*
issuance émission *f*
issue émission *f*; [*of notes*] mise en circulation *f*
to **issue** [*cheques, bank notes, shares*] émettre

to **issue a bond** émettre un emprunt, lancer un emprunt
issue of a certificate délivrance d'un certificat *f*
issue of a credit card délivrance de carte bancaire *f*
issue price prix d'émission *m*
issued securities titres émis *mpl*
issued (share) capital capital social *m*
issuer émetteur *m*
issuer of a draft émetteur d'une traite *m*
issuing [*of loans, notes, payment instruments*] émission *f*
issuing bank banque d'émission *f*
issuing house banque de placement *f*, institut d'émission *m*
issuing of an insurance policy édition d'un contrat d'assurance *f*
item poste *m*

J

jobber's turn profit du courtier *m*
joint account compte joint *m*
joint and several debtor débiteur solidaire *m*
joint and several guarantee cautionnement solidaire *m*
joint and several guarantor garant solidaire *m*
joint debtor codébiteur *m*
joint holder codétenteur *m*

joint-stock bank banque
  commerciale *f*
jointly and severally
  conjointement et solidairement

jumbo trade opération jumbo *f*
junk bond obligation de
  pacotille *f*

K

K (1000) KF, kilofranc
key index indice clé *m*

key rate taux directeur *m*
Keynesian keynésien

L

lack of funds manque de fonds *m*;
  for lack of funds faute de
  provision
land bank crédit foncier *m*
last trading day dernier jour de
  transaction *m*
late payment penalty indemnité
  de retard *f*
laundering [*of money*]

  blanchiment *m*
LBO (= Leveraged Buy-Out)
  rachat d'entreprises avec un fort
  levier financier *m*
L/C (= Letter of Credit) l/c *f*
lead plomb *m*
to **lead manage** être chef de file de
lead manager chef de file *m*
lead time délai de réalisation *m*

lease bail *m*
to **lease** prendre à bail
lease contract contrat de bail *m*
leasehold droit au bail *m*
lease-purchase contract contrat de crédit-bail *m*
lease with purchase option location avec option d'achat *f*
leasing location-bail *f*, crédit-bail *m*
legal tender: to be legal tender avoir cours
to **lend** prêter
to **lend against securities** prêter sur titres
to **lend at interest** prêter à intérêt
lender prêteur *m*, organisme prêteur *m*
lender of the last resort prêteur de dernier recours *m*
lending concours *m*, concours bancaire *m*
lending *adj* prêteur
lending bank banquier prêteur *m*
lending rate taux de prêt *m*
lending syndicate syndicat bancaire *m*
less moins
lessor bailleur *m*
letter of comfort lettre de confort *f*
letter of confirmation lettre de confirmation *f*
letter of credit lettre de crédit *f*
letter of guarantee lettre de garantie *f*
to **level out** plafonner
levelling out plafonnement *m*
leverage effet de levier *m*
to **leverage a deal** faire une opération à effet de levier
leveraged: *leveraged buy-out* rachat d'entreprises avec un fort

levier financier *m*; *highly leveraged transaction* transaction à fort effet de levier *f*
levy at source prélèvement libératoire *m*
liabilities passif *m*, passif du bilan *m*; [*commitments*] engagements *mpl*
liability management gestion du passif *f*
LIBOR (= London Inter-Bank Offered Rate) LIBOR *m*
licenced deposit-taking institution institution autorisée à recevoir des dépôts *f*
lien droit de gage *m*
life assurance *Br* assurance-vie *f*
life assurance and savings products produits assurance vie et capitalisation *mpl*
life capitalization capitalisation viagère *f*
life insurance assurance-vie *f*
life insurance policy assurance-vie *f*
life policy assurance-vie *f*
lifetime [*of an option*] durée de vie *f*
to **lift a mortgage from** déshypothéquer
limit limite *f*; *to put a regulatory limit on* plafonner réglementairement
limit order ordre limité *m*
limited profit gain limité *m*
limited risk risque limité *m*
line of credit ligne de crédit *f*
liquid liquide
liquid asset actif liquide *m*
liquid assets liquidités *fpl*, disponibilités *fpl*
liquid resources moyens liquides *mpl*

to **liquidate a position** liquider une position

liquidation date date de liquidation *f*

liquidation of a position liquidation d'une position *f*

liquidation of assets liquidation des biens *f*

liquidator liquidateur *m*

liquidity liquidité *f*

liquidity guarantee garantie de solvabilité *f*

liquidity ratio ratio de liquidité *m*, coefficient de liquidité *m*

list [*on Stock Exchange*] cote *f*

to **list on the Stock Exchange** introduire en Bourse; [*shares*] émettre en Bourse

list of bills for discount bordereau d'escompte *m*

list of drawings [*of money*] liste des tirages *f*

list of shareholders liste des actionnaires *f*

listed stock valeurs cotées *fpl*

listing [*on Stock Exchange*] introduction en Bourse *f*

listing requirements conditions d'admission à la cote *fpl*

load funds fonds avec frais d'acquisition *mpl*

loan [*lent*] crédit *m*, prêt *m*; [*borrowed*] crédit *m*, emprunt *m*

loan against securities prêt sur titres *m*

loan agreement contrat de prêt *m*

loan applicant demandeur de crédit *m*

loan application dossier de (demande de) crédit *m*

loan at interest prêt à intérêts *m*

loan book encours de crédit *m*

loan contract convention de prêt *f*, accord de prêt *m*

loan facility facilité de prêt *f*

loan note titre d'obligation *m*, titre de créance *m*

loan notes obligations *fpl*

loan portfolio management gestion du portefeuille de prêts *f*

loan repayment remboursement de prêt *m*

loan risk cover couverture du risque de crédit *f*

loan shark usurier *m*

loan stock obligations *fpl*

loan syndication syndication de prêt *f*

loan to value rapport entre le capital restant dû et la valeur du bien financé *m*

loans outstanding concours *m*, encours des créances *m*

local bill effet sur place *m*

local currency monnaie locale *f*

local (trader) négociateur individuel de parquet *m*

lock-in à cliquet

to **lock in a hedge** immobiliser une couverture

locking in a hedge immobilisation d'une couverture *f*

to **lodge security** déposer une caution

logo logo *m*

Lombard rate taux Lombard *m*

long [*bill*] effet à longue échéance *m*

long: to go long prendre une position longue; *to be long* jouer à la hausse

long bond titre long *m*

long-dated bill traite à longue échéance *f*

long-dated security titre à longue échéance *m*

long lease bail emphytéotique *m*

long maturity échéance éloignée *f*

long position position longue *f*, position acheteur *f*

long rate taux long *m*

long term long terme *m*

long-term *adj* à long terme

long-term bond market marché des obligations à long terme *m*

long-term bond rate taux long obligataire *m*

long-term borrowings emprunts à long terme *mpl*

long-term capital capitaux permanents *mpl*

long-term credit crédit (à) long terme *m*

long-term credit bank banque de crédit à long terme *f*, crédit national *m*

long-term debt endettement à (long) terme *m*

long-term financing financement à long terme *m*

long-term funds ressources à long terme *fpl*

long-term indebtedness endettement à long terme *m*

long-term interest rate taux d'intérêt à long terme *m*

long-term investment placement à long terme *m*; [*equity holding*] immobilisation financière *f*

long-term loan prêt à long terme *m*, emprunt à long terme *m*

long-term rate taux à long terme *m*, taux long *m*

long-term yield rendement long *m*

to **lose ground against the franc** déprécier contre le franc

to **lose on** perdre sur

loss manque à gagner *m*, perte *f*; *at a loss* à perte; *to show a loss* enregistrer une perte; *to record a loss* enregistrer une perte

loss-leading price prix d'appel *m*

loss-making déficitaire

loss of interest perte d'intérêts *f*

loss of profit perte de bénéfice *f*

loss of value dévalorisation *f*

lost and stolen card office centre d'opposition *m*

lot lot *m*, quotité *f*

lot size quotité de négociation *f*, unité de transaction *f*; *to have a lot size of* porter sur

to **lower** [*rates*] abaisser; [*value of a share*] déprécier

lower limit borne basse *f*

lump sum forfait *m*, somme forfaitaire *f*; *in a lump sum* forfaitairement

lump-sum *adj* forfaitaire

M

M3 money supply masse monétaire M3 *f*
made out in libellé en
made out to [*cheque*] libellé à l'ordre de
made out to bearer libellé au porteur
magnetic stripe ligne magnétique *f*
mail transfer virement par courrier *m*
major bank grande banque *f*
to **make out a cheque** libeller un chèque
to **make out a statement of account** relever un compte
to **make out to the order of** libeller à l'ordre de
make-up date date de situation *f*
to **manage an account** gérer un compte
to **manage assets** gérer des actifs, régir des biens
management pilotage *m*
management buy-in rachat d'entreprise par des repreneurs extérieurs *m*
management buyout rachat d'entreprise par les salariés *m*
management by objectives gestion par objectifs *f*
management fee commission de gestion *f*
manager [*of a branch*] directeur

m; *account manager* chargé de compte *m*
margin [*in securities trading*] dépôt de garantie *m*, marge *f*; [*general sense*] marge *f*
margin call appel de marge *m*, appel de garantie *m*
margin default défaut de couverture *m*
margin requirement niveau de dépôt requis *m*
margin trading opérations sur marge *fpl*
mark-to-market principle principe mark to market *m*
to **mark to market** comptabiliser au prix de marché, actualiser
market marché *m*; *after market* après Bourse *f*
market *adj* [*Stock Market*] boursier
market activities activités de marché *fpl*
market call appel au marché *m*
market capitalization capitalisation boursière *f*
market close clôture du marché *f*; *at market close* en clôture
market commentator chroniquier boursier *m*
market conditions conditions de marché *fpl*
market crisis crise boursière *f*, choc boursier *m*

market deregulation décloisonnement des marchés *m*

market economy économie des marchés *f*

market equilibrium équilibre des marchés *m*

market fluctuation errement du marché *m*

market instrument instrument de marché *m*

market maker teneur du marché *m*, mainteneur de marché *m*

market making tenue de marché *f*

market member membre de marché *m*

market order ordre au mieux *m*; **at the market order** ordre au mieux

market participant participant de marché *m*

market phenomena phénomènes de marché *mpl*

market player intervenant *m*, acteur de marché *m*

market price cours du marché *m*; *at (the) market price* au cours du marché

market rate taux du marché *m*

market regulation réglementation de marché *f*

market risk risque de marché *m*

market rules règles de marché *fpl*

market setbacks déboires boursiers *mpl*

market size taille boursière *f*

market value valeur boursière *f*, valeur marchande *f*

market trader teneur de marché *m*

market trend conjoncture boursière *f*

market volatility volatilité des marchés *f*

marketable security valeur mobilière de placement *f*

marketization marchéisation *f*

marking to market valorisation au prix de marché *f*

matched trade opération confirmée *f*

mathematical financial model modèle de mathématique financière *m*

mathematical formula formule de calcul *f*

maturity échéance *f*, maturité *f*

maturity date date d'échéance *f*, terme d'échéance *m*

maturity value valeur à l'échéance *f*

maximum amount montant maximum *m*

MBI (= Management Buy-In) rachat d'entreprise par des repreneurs extérieurs *m*

MBO (= Management BuyOut) RES *m*

MBO (= Management By Objectives) gestion par objectifs *f*

means of payment moyens de paiement *mpl*

medical insurance assurance pour les frais médicaux *f*, assurance santé *f*

medium term moyen terme *m*

medium-term *adj* à moyen terme

medium-term credit crédit (à) moyen terme *m*

medium-term credit bank banque de crédit à moyen terme *f*

medium-term financing financement à moyen terme *m*

medium-term indebtedness endettement à moyen terme *m*

medium-term visibility visibilité
à moyen terme *f*
medium- to long-term moyen,
long terme, MLT
member [*of insurance scheme*]
cotisant *m*
merchant bank banque
d'affaires *f*
merchant banker banquier
d'affaires *m*
to **merge** fusionner
merger fusion *f*
method of payment modalité de
paiement *f*, mode de paiement *m*
mine/yours j'achète/je vends
to **minimize one's losses**
minimiser sa perte
minimum amount montant
minimum *m*
minimum quantity quantité
minimale *f*
minimum rates taux minima *mpl*
mixed credits crédits mixtes *mpl*
mixed portfolio portefeuille
diversifié *m*
MMFs (= Money Market Funds)
sicav monétaires *fpl*
monetary monétaire
monetary aggregate agrégat
monétaire *m*
monetary area zone monétaire *f*
monetary asset actif monétaire *m*
monetary base base monétaire *f*
monetary economics économie
monétaire *f*
monetary equilibrium équilibre
monétaire *m*
monetary expansion création
monétaire *f*
monetary fluctuations
mouvements monétaires *mpl*
monetary growth croissance
monétaire *f*

monetary parity parité des
monnaies *f*
monetary standard étalon
monétaire *m*
monetary unit unité monétaire *f*
monetization monétisation *f*
to **monetize** monétiser
money argent *m*; *in the money*
dans les cours; *at the money* à
parité; *out of the money* hors
des cours; *slightly in the money*
faiblement dans les cours
money-centre bank grande
banque de dépôt de New York *f*
money demand demande de
monnaie *f*
money laundering blanchiment de
l'argent *m*
money market place monétaire *f*,
marché monétaire *m*
money market fund fonds
commun de placement en titres
du marché monétaire *m*, sicav de
trésorerie *f*
money market funds = sicav
monétaires *fpl*
money market mutual funds *Am*
= sicavs monétaires *fpl*
money market rate taux de
marché monétaire *m*, TMM *m*
money market transactions
opérations sur le marché
monétaire *fpl*
money multiplier multiplicateur
monétaire *m*
money of account monnaie de
compte *f*
money order mandat(-poste) *m*
money supply masse
monétaire *f*
money trader cambiste *mf*
to **monitor** contrôler
monies deniers *mpl*

monometallism
monométallisme *m*

monthly mensuel

monthly *adv* mensuellement

monthly instalment acompte
mensuel *m*, mensualité *f*

monthly return situation
mensuelle *f*

monthly settlement règlement
mensuel *m*

moratorium moratoire *m*

moratorium on payment
suspension de paiements *f*

mortgage [*for property purchase*]
crédit immobilier *m*; [*money
raised on property*] hypothèque *f*

mortgage *adj* hypothécaire

to **mortgage an asset** hypothéquer
un bien

mortgage banking crédit
hypothécaire *m*

mortgage-backed bond
obligation représentative de
créances hypothécaires *f*

mortgage bond obligation
hypothécaire *f*

mortgage customer emprunteur
immobilier *m*

mortgage debt dette foncière *f*

mortgage deed acte
hypothécaire *m*

mortgage loan crédit
hypothécaire *m*

mortgage market marché
hypothécaire *m*

mortgage rate taux de crédit
immobilier *m*

mortgage repayments
remboursements de prêt
hypothécaire *mpl*

mortgageable hypothécable

mortgaged property bien
hypothéqué *m*

mortgagee créancier
hypothécaire *m*

mortgagor débiteur
hypothécaire *m*

motor insurance assurance auto *f*

movement of capital mouvement
des capitaux *m*

movement of funds mouvement
de fonds *m*

multicurrency multidevise

multicurrency account compte
multidevise *m*

multicurrency clause clause
multidevise *f*

multicurrency loan prêt
multidevise *m*

multicurrency management
gestion multidevise *f*

multifunction card carte
multiprestataire *f*, carte
multifonction *f*

multifunction terminal terminal
multifonction *m*

multiple component facility
crédit multidevise à utilisation
multiple *m*

mutual bank banque mutualiste *f*

mutual fund société
d'investissement à capital
variable *f*, SICAV *f*, Opcvm *m*

**mutual guarantee insurance
company** société de caution
mutuelle *f*

mutual investment fund fonds
commun de placement *m*,
FCP *m*

mutualization of risk
mutualisation des risques *f*

N

naked option option découverte *f*

naked sale vente nue *f*

naked warrant warrant découvert *m*

narrow market marché étroit *m*, marché peu liquide *m*

narrowing of margins contraction des marges *f*

natural hedging autocouverture *f*

NBD (= Next Business Day) prochain jour ouvrable *m*

near bank presque banque *f*

near money quasi-monnaie *f*

near month échéance proche *f*

negative equity excédent d'une dette mobilière par rapport à la valeur amoindrie de la propriété pour laquelle elle a été contractée *m*

negotiability négociabilité *f*

negotiable négociable

negotiable CD certificat de dépôt négociable *m*, CDN *m*

negotiable certificate of deposit certificat de dépôt négociable *m*

negotiable debt instruments titres de créances négociables *mpl*

negotiable instrument titre négociable *m*

negotiable paper papier négociable *m*

to **negotiate** négocier

net montant net *m*

net *adj* net

net assets actif net *m*

net banking revenue produit net bancaire *m*

net cash position trésorerie nette *f*

net dividend dividende net *m*

net loss perte nette *f*

net margin rentabilité nette *f*

net present value valeur actuelle nette *f*

net profit bénéfice net *m*

net profit after tax résultat de l'exercice *m*

net revenue collecte nette *f*

net settlement règlement net *m*

net total montant net *m*

net variance écart net *m*

net worth actif net *m*, situation nette *f*; [*of individual*] patrimoine *m*

net worth *adj* patrimonial

network operators opérateurs de réseaux *mpl*

netting [*in foreign exchange trading*] compensation *f*

new borrowings nouveaux emprunts *mpl*

new issue [*of shares*] nouvelle émission *f*

new issue market marché des nouvelles émissions *m*

new issuer nouvel émetteur *m*

new savings épargne nouvelle *f*

niche activities activités sur des niches *fpl*

NIF (= Note Issuance Facility) facilité d'émission de billets *f*

night safe coffre de nuit *m*

Nikkei index indice Nikkei *m*

no-load [*funds*] sans frais d'acquisition

no-loss investment produit garanti *m*

nominal bond obligation fictive *f*

nominal capital capital nominal *m*

nominal interest rate taux d'intérêt nominal *m*

nominal rate taux nominal *m*

nominee company prête-nom *m*

non-bank non-banque *f*

non-bank bank établissement para-bancaire *m*

non-bank borrower emprunteur non bancaire *m*

non-bank financial institution institution financière non bancaire *f*, IFNB *f*

non-banking service provider prestataire non-banque *m*

non-convertible inconvertible

non-exchangeable inéchangeable

non-executive director administrateur indépendant de la gestion *m*

non-interest bearing non rémunéré

non-intervention non-ingérence *f*

non-liquid asset actif illiquide *m*

non-negotiable cheque chèque non endossable *m*

non-payment non-paiement *m*, refus de paiement *m*; *for non-payment* faute de paiement

non-performance of a contract inexécution d'un contrat *f*

non-performing loan prêt en souffrance *m*

non-performing loans encours douteux *mpl*

non-profit-making à but non lucratif

non-recourse à forfait

non-repayment non-remboursement *m*

non-transferability incessibilité *f*, intransférabilité *f*

non-transferable incessible, intransférable

non-voting stock certificats d'investissement *mpl*

nostro account compte nostro *m*

not-for-profit *Am* à but non lucratif

not to order clause non à ordre

notarized notarié

note issuance facility facilité d'émission de billets *f*

notes in circulation billets en circulation *mpl*

notice date délai de notification *m*

notice of withdrawal avis de retrait *m*

notional contract contrat notionnel *m*

NPV (= No Par Value) SVN

NPV (= Net Present Value) VAN *f*

null and void nul et non-applicable

numbered account contremarque *f*

NYSE (= New York Stock Exchange) Wall Street

O

obligation to pay engagement de payer *m*

to **obtain a return on investments** rentabiliser des investissements

off-balance sheet hors bilan; [*adjustment*] extra-comptable

off-balance sheet product produit de hors bilan *m*

off-balance sheet transactions opérations de hors bilan *fpl*

off-exchange quotation system système extra-boursier de cotation des titres *m*

off-market marché extra-boursier *m*

to **offset a loss** compenser une perte

offshore bank banque off shore *f*

offshore financial market place off shore *f*

offshore investment placement off shore *m*

offer offre *f*

offer price cours vendeur *m*, prix vendeur *m*

official brokerage courtage officiel *m*

official list cote officielle *f*

official rate cours officiel *m*, taux officiel *m*

Old Lady of Threadneedle Street Banque d'Angleterre *f*

online banking bancatique *f*

to **open an account** ouvrir un compte

to **open a position** ouvrir une position

open cheque chèque non barré *m*

open-end investment fund *Am* SICAV *f*

open-ended credit crédit à durée indéterminée *m*

open interest intérêt du marché *m*

open order ordre à exécution *m*

open outcry system système de criée *m*

open position position ouverte *f*

opening [*of account, Stock Exchange*] ouverture *f*

opening hours heures d'ouverture *fpl*

opening of a position ouverture d'une position *f*

opening price cours d'ouverture *m*

opening time heure d'ouverture *f*

opening up of markets ouverture des marchés *f*

operating expenses charges d'exploitation *fpl*

operating lease bail d'exploitation *m*

operating profit résultat d'exploitation *m*

operating provision provision d'exploitation *f*

opportunity loss manque à gagner potentiel *m*

option option *f*

option holder détenteur d'une option *m*

option on an option option sur option *f*

option on shares option sur actions *f*

option right droit d'option *m*

option series série d'options *f*

option spread écart de prime *m*

option to buy option d'achat *f*

option to sell option de vente *f*

options contract contrat d'options *m*

options desk desk d'options *m*

options trading négociations à prime *fpl*

order ordre *m*; *to the order of* à l'ordre de

order at the closing price ordre au dernier cours *m*

order at the prevailing price ordre au cours *m*

order execution slip bordereau d'exécution *m*

order form bulletin de commande *m*

order-giver donneur d'ordre *m*

order to pay ordonnance de paiement *f*, commandement à payer *m*

order to sell ordre de vente *m*

orderly market marché ordonné *m*

ordinary creditor créancier ordinaire *m*

ordinary share action ordinaire *f*

OTC market (= Over-The-Counter) marché hors cote *m*

outcry: by open outcry à la criée

outflow sortie *f*

outflows of capital sorties de capitaux *fpl*

outlay mise de fonds *f*

outstanding impayé

outstanding cheques chèques en circulation *mpl*

outstanding debt créance à recouvrer *f*, impayé *m*

outstanding interest intérêts échus *mpl*

overbanked surbancarisé

overdraft découvert d'un compte *m*; *to go into overdraft* passer en découvert

overdraft facility ligne de découvert *f*

overdraft limit plafond de découvert *m*

overdraft loan prêt à découvert *m*, avance en compte débiteur *f*

to **overdraw** tirer à découvert; *to overdraw one's account* tirer à découvert

overdrawn à découvert, désapprovisionné; *to go overdrawn* passer en découvert; *your account is overdrawn* votre compte est débiteur

overdrawn account compte à découvert *m*, compte débiteur *m*

overdue interest intérêts échus et non payés *mpl*

overexposed: to be overexposed [*of bank*] courir trop de risques

over-gearing surendettement *m*

overhead(s) frais généraux *mpl*

overheating [*of economy*] surchauffe *f*

over-indebtedness surendettement *m*

overnight au jour le jour, J.J.

overnight loan prêt au jour le jour *m*

overnight money argent au jour le jour *m*

141

overnight rate taux de l'argent au jour le jour *m*, TJJ *m*
over-offering sur-offre *f*
overseas account compte à l'étranger *m*
overseas investment investissement à l'étranger *m*
overseas investor investisseur étranger *m*
oversubscribed sursouscrit
over-the-counter market marché hors cote *m*
to **owe** devoir
own funds fonds propres *mpl*
own-funds financing financement sur fonds propres *m*

P

paid [*invoice*] payé
paid in advance payé d'avance
paid-up share capital capital versé *m*, actions libérées *fpl*
paper money papier-monnaie *m*, monnaie de papier *f*
paper transactions masse papier *f*
paperless handling of securities dématérialisation *f*
par pair *m*; *above par* au-dessus du pair; *at par* au pair; *close to par* au voisinage de la parité; *below par* au-dessous du pair
par value nominal *m*, valeur nominale *f*; *no par value* sans valeur nominale
parallel currency monnaie parallèle *f*
pari passu clause clause pari passu *f*

Paris market place de Paris *f*
Paris Stock Exchange watchdog Commission des opérations de Bourse *f*, COB *f*
parity parité *f*
partial takeover bid OPA partielle *f*
partially: *to partially close (out) a position* clore une position en partie
passbook carnet d'épargne *m*
password mot de passe *m*
to **pay** payer; [*into account, interest*] verser; [*pay out, spend*] débourser; [*employee*] rémunérer; [*invoice*] régler; *to pay in advance* payer à l'avance, anticiper un paiement; *to pay in cash* régler au comptant; *to pay on the due date* honorer ses échéances

to **pay a dividend** distribuer un dividende

to **pay an annuity** servir une rente

to **pay a premium** acquitter une prime

to **pay a rate** verser un taux

to **pay at sight** payer à vue

to **pay back** rembourser

to **pay in** [*sum of money: customer*] verser; [*bank*] encaisser

to **pay money in** faire un versement

to **pay money into an account** approvisionner un compte

to **pay in a cheque** déposer un chèque

to **pay off a creditor** désintéresser un créancier

to **pay off a debt** amortir une dette, liquider une dette

to **pay off a loan** rembourser; [*make final payment*] finir de rembourser

to **pay out** décaisser

payback period période de récupération *f*

pay day [*on Stock Exchange*] jour de règlement *m*

pay-in versement *m*; *to make a pay-in* faire un versement

pay-in slip bordereau de remise *m*, feuille de versement *f*

pay to bearer payez au porteur

pay to bearer clause clause au porteur *f*

payable payable, exigible; [*charge*] décaissable

payable at maturity payable à l'échéance

payable at the bank payable à la banque

payable in advance payable par anticipation

payable in arrears payable à terme échu

payee bénéficiaire *mf*, accrédité *m*; [*of bill of exchange*] preneur *m*

payer payeur *m*

paying bank domiciliataire *m*, établissement payeur *m*

paying-in [*by customer*] versement *m*; [*by bank*] encaissement *m*

paying-in date date d'encaissement *f*

paying-in slip bordereau de versement *m*, bordereau d'opération *m*

paying off amortissement *m*

paying out déboursement *m*

payment paiement *m*; [*into account, of interest*] versement *m*; [*spending*] déboursement *m*; [*of employee*] rémunération *f*; [*of invoice*] règlement *m*

payment advice avis de paiement *m*

payment at maturity paiement à échéance *m*

payment at sight paiement à vue *m*

payment by card paiement par carte *m*

payment by cheque règlement par chèque *m*

payment card carte de paiement *f*

payment date date de paiement *f*; [*of interest, into account*] date de versement *f*

payment day jour de paiement *m*

payment in arrears paiement arriéré *m*, paiement à terme échu *m*

payment in cash paiement comptant *m*, règlement au comptant *m*

payment in full paiement intégral *m*

payment instrument instrument de paiement *m*

payment of a dividend distribution de dividende *f*, passation d'un dividende *f*

payment order ordre de paiement *m*

payment slip bordereau de paiement *m*

payment system système de paiement *m*

payment term délai de paiement *m*

payments management gestion des incidents de paiement *f*

payments risk risque de paiement *m*

payslip bulletin de salaire *m*

PBDIT (= Profit Before Depreciation, Interest and Tax) EBE *m*

penal rate taux d'usure *m*

penalty clause clause pénale *f*

pension retraite *f*, pension *f*

pension fund caisse de retraite *f*, fonds de pension *m*

pension plan régime de retraite *m*

pension scheme système de retraite *m*

pension supplement complément de retraite *m*

PEP (= Personal Equity Plan) PEA *m*

per cent pour cent

percentage pourcentage *m*

percentage point point *m*

performance bond caution de bonne fin *f*

performance ratio coefficient d'exploitation *m*

performing loan crédit "sain" *m*

period of grace délai de grâce *m*

period of validity délai de validité *m*, durée de validité *f*

personal account manager chargé de clientèle grand public *m*

personal assets patrimoine *m*

personal equity plan plan d'épargne en actions *m*

personal estate bien mobilier *m*

personal financial statement état de fortune *m*

personal loan crédit personnel *m*, prêt personnalisé *m*

personal wealth statement état de fortune *m*

petrodollar pétro-dollar *m*

phantom withdrawal retrait fantôme (dû à une erreur électronique) *m*

physical market marché du physique *m*

PIBOR (= Paris InterBank Offered Rate) PIBOR *m*, TIOP *m*; *one-month PIBOR* PIBOR 1 mois

to **pick up 10 billion** lever 10 milliards

picture cheque image-chèque *f*

piggy-backing portage *m*

PIN (= Personal Identification Number) code confidentiel *m*

PIN number code confidentiel *m*, numéro confidentiel *m*

pink sheet securities valeurs de second rang *fpl*

pit: the pit [*at Stock Exchange*] la corbeille

to **place** [*order, securities*] placer

to **place an order for sth** passer commande de qch

to **place an order with sb** passer commande à qn

place of issue lieu d'émission *m*

place of payment lieu de paiement *m*

placing of an order passation de commande *f*

placing of an order on the Stock Exchange passation d'un ordre de Bourse *f*

plain vanilla interest rate swap échange simple de taux d'intérêt *m*

plastic money cartes de crédit *fpl*

to **play sth** jouer qch

to **play the market** jouer en Bourse

player acteur *m*

pledge nantissement *m*

pledge over business assets nantissement de fonds de commerce *m*

pledged gagé, nanti

pledged as security placé en garantie

pledgee gagiste *mf*

pledgor gageur *m*

point [*in rate changes*] point *m*; *to* **drop/rise two points** perdre/gagner deux points

point of sale terminal terminal point de vente *m*

poison pill mesures prises par une société afin de se rendre peu attirante pour une OPA *fpl*

portfolio portefeuille *m*

portfolio management gestion de portefeuille *f*

POS terminal (= Point of Sale) TPV *m*

position position *f*; [*for bank teller*] guichet de banque *m*

position limit limite de position *f*

position on an account état de compte *m*

position taking prise de position *f*

possessory lien droit de retention *m*

to **post an amount** passer un montant

to **post security** déposer des garanties

to **postdate** [*cheque*] postdater

post office account compte postal *m*

post office cheque chèque postal *m*

post office cheque account compte chèque postal *m*

post office giro account compte courant postal *m*, CCP *m*

post office transfer virement postal *m*

potential loss perte potentielle *f*

potential profit gain potentiel *m*

pound livre *f*

power of attorney pouvoir *m*

to **predict a rise** prévoir une hausse

pre-emptive bid offre de préemption *f*

pre-emptive rights droits préférentiels de souscription *mpl*

preference share action à dividende prioritaire *f*, action privilégiée *f*

preferential creditor créancier privilégié *m*

preferred creditor créancier privilégié *m*

preferred debt dette privilégiée *f*, créance privilégiée *f*

preferred share *Am* action privilégiée *f*

premature exercise exercice prématuré *m*

premium prime *f*

premium rate taux de la prime *m*

prepaid prépayé, payé d'avance

prepaid card carte prépayée *f*

prepayment prépaiement *m*;
[*accounting*] charge constatée
d'avance *f*

to **present for collection** présenter
à l'encaissement

presentation date date de
présentation *f*

presentation for acceptance
présentation à l'acceptation *f*

presentation for payment
présentation au paiement *f*

presenting présentateur

president [*Am: of bank*] PDG *m*

pressure to sell pression à la vente *f*

price prix *m*; [*on Stock Exchange*]
cours *m*, cote *f*

price dissemination diffusion de
cours *f*

price-earnings ratio ratio cours-
bénéfice *m*

price fixing fixation des prix/
cours *f*

price fluctuation mouvement des
prix/cours *m*

price fluctuations variations de
prix/cours *fpl*

price formation formation du
cours *f*

price highs and lows sommets et
creux des cours *mpl*

price increase majoration de prix *f*

price inflation inflation des prix *f*

price instability instabilité des
prix/cours *f*

price limit order ordre à cours
limité *m*

price movement mouvement des
cours *m*

price of gold point de l'or *m*

price range fourchette de prix *f*,
gamme de prix *f*

price risk risque des cours *m*

price setting détermination des
prix/cours *f*

price spread écart des cours *m*

price stability stabilité des prix/
cours *f*

price variations variations de
prix/cours *fpl*

pricing curve courbe
d'évaluation *f*

primary debtor débiteur
principal *m*

primary dealer opérateur
principal de marché *m*, OPM *m*;
[*in government securities*]
spécialiste en valeurs du Trésor
mf, SVT *mf*

primary market marché primaire
m, marché du neuf *m*

primary option option mère *f*

prime rate taux préférentiel *m*

principal principal *m*; [*party in
transaction*] donneur d'ordre *m*,
commettant *m*; [*as opposed to
interest*] capital *m*

principal and interest principal et
intérêts *m*

principal debtor débiteur
principal *m*

principal debt créance
principale *f*

printed statement état imprimé *m*

prior debt dette antérieure *f*

private bank banque privée *f*

private banking banque privée *f*

private code code confidentiel *m*

private investor investisseur
privé *m*

private risk risque privé *m*

to **privatize** privatiser

to **process a cheque** traiter un
chèque

to **process in real time** exécuter en
temps réel

processing of transactions traitement transactionnel *m*

professional misconduct faute professionnelle *f*

professional secrecy secret professionnel *m*

profit gain *m*, bénéfice *m*, profit *m*; *to make a profit* réaliser un gain

profit-driven poussé par les profits

profit-making à but lucratif

profit opportunity occasion de profit *f*

profit-sharing scheme système d'intéressement aux bénéfices *m*

profitability rentabilité *f*

profitability ratio ratio de rentabilité *m*

profitable rentable, profitable; [*investment*] rémunérateur, fructueux

profitably [*to invest, etc.*] avec bénéfice

pro forma bill traite pro forma *f*

program trading program trading *m*

promissory note billet à ordre *m*, effet à ordre *m*

proof of debt affirmation de créance *f*

property immobilier *m*, propriété immobilière *f*

property assets biens immobiliers *mpl*, actifs immobiliers *mpl*

property commitment engagement immobilier *m*

property company société immobilière *f*

property debt créance immobilière *f*

property developer promoteur immobilier *m*

property development promotion immobilière *f*

property development loan crédit promoteur *m*

property finance financement immobilier *m*

property insurance assurance immobilière *f*

property investment placement immobilier *m*

property investment company société civile de placement immobilier *f*, SCPI *f*

property investment instrument véhicule d'investissement immobilier *m*

property lending prêts immobiliers *mpl*

property loan prêt immobilier *m*

property market marché immobilier *m*

property risk risque immobilier *m*

prospectus prospectus *m*

protest [*of bill*] protêt *m*; *without protest* sans protêt

to **protest** [*bill, etc.*] protester

protestable protestable

to **provide as surety/collateral** apporter en caution

to **provide funds** fournir des fonds

provision provision *f*

provision for bad debts provision pour créances douteuses *f*

provision for depreciation provision pour dépréciation *f*

provisions for country risk provisions sur risques-pays *fpl*

prudential prudentiel

public holiday jour chômé *m*, jour férié *m*

public offering offre publique de vente *f*, OPV *f*

public order book carnet d'ordres public *m*
public share offer offre publique de vente *f*, OPV *f*
purchase achat *m*
to **purchase** acheter; [*company*] racheter
purchase order [*on money markets*] ordre d'achat *m*; [*in commerce*] bon de commande *m*

purchaser acheteur *m*
purchasing power pouvoir d'achat *m*, capacité d'achat *f*
put put *m*
put and call option stellage *m*
put of twice more option d'achat doublée à la baisse *f*
put option put *m*, option de vente *f*

quarter trimestre *m*
quarterly trimestriel
quick turnover rotation rapide *f*
quid livre (sterling) *f*; [*on foreign exchange markets*] million de livres sterling *m*
quotation [*on Stock Exchange*] cotation *f*
quotation system système de cotation *m*
quote [*on Stock Exchange*] cotation *f*
to **quote** coter
to **quote a maturity** coter une

échéance
to **quote a month** coter une échéance
to **quote a price** faire un prix, indiquer un prix; [*on Stock Exchange*] afficher un prix
to **quote an expiry** coter une échéance
quoted [*company*] coté
quoted on the Stock Exchange coté en Bourse
quoted securities valeurs cotées *fpl*, valeurs de Bourse *fpl*

R

raid raid *m*

raider prédateur *m*, raider *m*

to **raise money** mobiliser de l'argent

to **raise the ceiling on a credit** déplafonner un crédit

raising of funds mobilisation de fonds *f*, levée de fonds *f*

rally rally *m*

ramping achat important (d'actions) visant à en faire monter le prix *m*

range of strategies gamme de stratégies *f*

rate taux *m*; [*of exchange*] cours *m*, taux *m*; [*price*] tarif *m*

rate curve courbe des taux *f*

rate difference différence de cours *f*

rate differential différentiel de taux *m*

rate of claims [*in insurance*] sinistralité *f*

rate of exchange cours du change *m*, taux de change *m*

rate of interest taux d'intérêt *m*

rate of return taux de rendement *m*

rate volatility volatilité des taux *f*

rating rating *m*, score *m*, notation *f*

rating agency agence de notation financière *f*, agence de rating *f*

to **reach the expiry date** arriver à expiration

real balance solde réel *m*

real estate bien immobilier *m*

real estate loan prêt immobilier *m*

real interest rate taux d'intérêt réel *m*

real rate taux réel *m*

real terms: in real terms en termes réels

real time: in real time en temps réel

real-time settlement règlement en temps réel *m*

realizable securities valeurs réalisables *fpl*

to **realize the value of sth** réaliser la valeur de qch

recapitalization recapitalisation *f*

receipt reçu *m*, acquit de paiement *m*; [*of interest, etc.*] réception *f*

receipt of a dividend perception de dividende *f*

receivables créances *fpl*

to **receive a commission** percevoir une commission

to **receive a premium** encaisser un premium

to **receive a rate** recevoir un taux

to **receive interest** percevoir des intérêts

receiver administrateur judiciaire *m*

recession récession *f*

recipient allocataire *mf*

reciprocity réciprocité *f*

recognition as a bank agrément en qualité de banque *m*

recognized bank banque agréée *f*

reconciliation [*bank reconciliation*] rapprochement *m*

to **record transactions** comptabiliser des opérations

to **recoup one's investment** rentrer dans ses fonds

recourse recours *m*

recoverable debt créance recouvrable *f*

recovery [*economic*] reprise *f*

recovery of provisions reprise de provisions *f*

to **recredit** re-créditer

red: in the red dans le rouge; *to go into the red* passer dans le rouge

red clause credit crédit "red clause" *m*

red herring prospectus provisoire *m*

to **redeem** [*debt, policy, bond*] racheter; [*mortgage*] purger

redeemable [*share*] rachetable; [*loan*] amortissable

redemption [*of security, bond*] rachat *m*; [*of loan*] amortissement *m*

redemption date date d'échéance *f*

redemption method modalité d'amortissement *f*

redemption price prix de remboursement *m*

redemption value valeur de rachat *f*

rediscount réescompte *m*

to **rediscount** réescompter

rediscounting réescompte *m*

to **reduce the risk** alléger le risque

reduced rate taux réduit *m*

reduced rate loan prêt à taux réduit *m*

reduction in borrowings/gearing désendettement *m*

reduction of capital diminution du capital *f*

reference period période de référence *f*

reference rate taux de référence *m*

to **refill a card** recharger une carte

refillable electronic wallet porte-monnaie électronique rechargeable *m*

to **refinance** refinancer

refinance rate taux de refinancement *m*

refinancing [*of loan*] refinancement *m*

refinancing costs coût de refinancement *m*

refund remboursement *m*

to **refund** rembourser

refundable remboursable

refusal [*of a cheque*] rejet *m*

refusal of a loan refus de crédit *m*

to **refuse** [*cheque*] rejeter; [*loan*] refuser

regional exchange Bourse régionale *f*

regional manager directeur régional *m*

to **register a guarantee** enregistrer une garantie

register of shareholders livre d'actionnaires *m*

registered bank banque inscrite *f*

registered bond obligation nominative *f*

registered security titre nominatif *m*, valeur nominative *f*

registered share action nominative *f*

registered shares inscriptions nominatives *fpl*

registration of a mortgage inscription hypothécaire *f*

regulated market marché organisé *m*

regulation régulation *f*

regulator régulateur *m*

regulatory réglementaire

regulatory barrier barrière réglementaire *f*

regulatory body autorité réglementaire *f*

regulatory framework cadre réglementaire *m*

regulatory norms normes prudentielles *fpl*

regulatory ratio ratio réglementaire *m*

reinsurance réassurance *f*

to **reinsure** réassurer

reinsurer réassureur *m*

to **reinvest** réinvestir

reinvestment replacement *m*

reinvestment rate taux de replacement *m*

REIT (= Real Estate Investment Trust) *Am* société d'investissements immobiliers *f*

to **release funds into the market** irriguer le marché

remaining duration durée résiduelle *f*

to **remit** remettre

to **remit for collection** remettre à l'encaissement

to **remit for discount** remettre à l'escompte

remittance remise *f*; [*payment*] règlement *m*

remittance date date de remise *f*

remittance of bills remise d'effets *f*

remittance of funds remise de fonds *f*

to **remortgage** hypothéquer à nouveau

removal of tax (on) détaxation (de) *f*

to **renegotiate** renégocier

renegotiation renégociation *f*

to **renew a bill of exchange** renouveler une traite

to **renew a lease** reconduire un bail

to **renew an order** renouveler un ordre

renewable reconductible, renouvelable

renewal reconduction *f*, renouvellement *m*

renewal of a bank card renouvellement de carte bancaire *m*

to **rent** louer

rental agreement location simple *f*

re-order form demande de renouvellement *f*

to **repay** rembourser

repayable remboursable

repayment remboursement *m*

replacement capital capital remplacement *m*

to **replenish an account** approvisionner un compte

repo réméré *m*, pension *f*

repo rate taux de prise en pension *m*, taux des repos *m*

to **re-present** [*cheque*] représenter

to **re-present a bill for acceptance** représenter une traite à l'acceptation

repurchase rachat *m*; **with a repurchase option** pignoratif

repurchase agreement garantie de reprise *f*, réméré *m*, pension *f*

repurchase at a profit rachat gagnant *m*

repurchase right droit de rachat *m*

request for payment demande de règlement *f*

reregulation reréglementation *f*

to **reschedule** réaménager

to **reschedule a debt** rééchelonner une dette

rescheduling [*of debts*] rééchelonnement *m*

rescue sauvetage *m*

to **resell** revendre

reserve account compte de réserve *m*

reserve assets instruments de réserve *mpl*

reserve capital capital de réserve *m*

reserve currency monnaie de réserve *f*

reserve fund fonds de réserve *m*, fonds de garantie *m*

reserve requirement réserves obligatoires *fpl*

reserves réserves *fpl*

resistance level point de résistance *m*

to **restrict the supply of** [*a currency*] raréfier

to **restructure a debt** restructurer une dette

result résultat *m*

retail bank banque de détail *f*

retail banking banque de détail *f*

retail deposit petit dépôt *m*

retail order ordre de détail *m*

retail price index indice des prix de détail *m*

retained earnings résultat conservé *m*

retention of title clause clause de réserve de propriété *f*

to **retire a bond** racheter une obligation

retirement savings plan plan d'épargne-retraite *m*, PER *m*

retrocession rétrocession *f*

return [*yield*] rendement *m*

to **return a bill** retourner un effet

return on capital rentabilité du capital *f*

return on investment retour sur l'investissement *m*

returned cheque chèque retourné *m*

revaluation réévaluation *f*

revaluation reserve écarts de réévaluation *mpl*

to **revalue** réévaluer, revaloriser

revenue revenu *m*; [*from shares, property*] rentes *fpl*; *the Revenue* le Fisc *m*

reversionary owner nu-propriétaire *m*

reversionary ownership nue-propriété *f*

reversionary pension pension de réversion *f*

revocability révocabilité *f*

revocable [*loan*] révocable

revolving credit crédit permanent *m*, crédit revolving *m*

revolving line of credit crédit renouvelable *m*

right of assignment droit d'attribution *m*

right of lien droit de gage *m*

rights issue émission de droits de souscription *f*, augmentation de capital (avec droits de souscription préférentiels) *f*

ring: the ring [*at Stock Exchange*] la corbeille

to **rise** [*shares, rates*] s'inscrire en hausse; *to rise by (18%)*

s'inscrire en hausse de (18%)
rising [*market*] orienté à la hausse
risk risque *m*; *a bad risk* un
mauvais client, un client risqué
risk analysis étude du risque *f*
risk-analysis professionals
professionnels de l'analyse des
risques *mpl*
risk asset ratio coefficient de
solvabilité *m*, ratio Cooke *m*
risk asymmetry dissymétrie des
risques *f*
risk-averse averse au risque
risk control contrôle des risques *m*
risk diversification diversification
des risques *f*
risk exposure exposition aux
risques *f*
risk insurance assurance de
risques *f*
risk management gestion des
risques *f*
risk management strategy
stratégie de risques *f*
risk management tool instrument
de maîtrise du risque *m*

risk monitoring suivi des risques
m, surveillance des risques *f*
risk-reward ratio ratio risque-
rentabilité *m*
risk spread répartition des risques *f*
risky risqué, aléatoire
rocket scientist personne chargée
de l'élaboration d'instruments
financiers complexes *f*
ROI (= Return On Investment)
retour sur l'investissement *m*
to **roll over** [*loan*] renouveler
rolled over [*loan*] renouvelé
rollover credit crédit à taux
révisable *m*
rollover loan crédit à taux
révisable *m*
to **round off** arrondir
rubber cheque chèque en bois *m*,
chèque sans provision *m*
**RUF (= Revolving Underwriting
Facility)** facilité avec
engagement de prise ferme *f*
run on the dollar spéculation
contre le dollar *f*

S

safe custody garde en dépôt *f*
safe custody account dépôt-
titres *m*

safe custody fees droits de
garde *mpl*
safe deposit box lock box *m*

safe deposit box rental location de coffres *f*

safe investment valeur refuge *f*

safety deposit box coffre-fort *m*

salary slip bulletin de salaire *m*

sale vente *f*

sale and leaseback cession-bail *f*

sale and repurchase agreement mise en pension *f*, réméré *m*

sales commission commission de vente *f*

sales contract bordereau de vente *m*

same-day value valeur jour *f*

Samurai bond obligation étrangère libellée en yens *f*

to **satisfy one's creditors** satisfaire ses créanciers

to **save** épargner

save as you earn épargne salariale *f*

saver épargnant

saving épargne *f*

savings épargne *f*; [*in costs*] économies *fpl*

savings account compte d'épargne *m*

savings and loan association *Am* caisse d'épargne-logement *f*

savings and loan association account *Am* compte épargne-logement *m*

savings bank banque d'épargne *f*, caisse d'épargne *f*

savings bank deposit book livret de caisse d'épargne *m*

savings bonds bons de capitalisation *mpl*

savings book carnet d'épargne *m*

savings certificate bon d'épargne *m*

savings club club d'épargne *m*

savings deposit dépôt d'épargne *m*

savings initiative effort d'épargne *m*

savings plan plan d'épargne *m*

savings product produit d'épargne *m*

savings rate taux d'épargne *m*

savings society société d'épargne *f*

SC (= Service Charge) frais d'opération *mpl*

scale of interest échelle d'intérêts *f*

scalper spéculateur sur variation minimale *m*

scoring grid grille de score *f*

scrip dividend dividende d'action *m*

scrip issue émission d'actions gratuites *f*

SDR (= Special Drawing Rights) DTS *mpl*

seasonal effect effet saisonnier *m*

SEC (= Securities and Exchange Commission) ≈ COB *m*

second mortgage hypothèque de deuxième rang *f*

secondary bank banque secondaire *f*

secondary market marché secondaire *m*, marché de l'occasion *m*

secondary offering reclassement de titres *m*

to **secure** cautionner; *to secure (on)* nantir (sur)

to **secure a loan** garantir un emprunt

secured creditor créancier nanti *m*

secured debt créance garantie *f*

secured loan emprunt garanti *m*

securities titres *mpl*, valeurs mobilières *fpl*

securities-backed loan avance sur titres *f*

securities certificate certificat de titres *m*

securities dealing opérations sur titres *fpl*, OST *fpl*

securities department service des titres *m*, administration des titres *f*

securities deposit dépôt-titres *m*

securities house société de Bourse *f*, maison de titres *f*

securities houses institutions article 99 *fpl*

securities issue émission de titres *f*

securities issued valeurs émises *fpl*

securities market marché des titres *m*, marché de valeurs mobilières *m*

securities portfolio portefeuille de titres *m*

securities trading opérations sur titres *fpl*, OST *fpl*

securities underwriting prise ferme d'une émission de titres *f*

securitization titrisation *f*

to **securitize** [*loan*] titriser

securitized debt créance titrisée *f*

securitized lending prêts titrisés *mpl*

security titre *m*, valeur mobilière *f*; [*for loan*] caution *f*; [*of premises, etc.*] sécurité *f*

security guard [*for transport of money*] convoyeur de fonds *m*

security manager responsable de sécurité *mf*

seed capital capital de départ *m*

see-saw effect effet balançoire *m*

seizure of property saisie immobilière *f*

self-service bank banque libre-service *f*

self-service banking banque libre-service *f*

self-service machine distributeur automatique de billets *m*

to **sell** vendre

to **sell for cash** vendre au comptant

to **sell forward** vendre à terme

to **sell off cheaply** brader

to **sell one's shares in a company** retirer sa participation d'une société

to **sell out** retirer sa participation d'une société

to **sell short** vendre à découvert, jouer à la baisse

sell contract ordre de vente *m*

sell order injonction à la vente *f*, ordre de vente *m*

seller vendeur *m*; *to be a seller* se porter vendeur

semi-annual semestriel

senior clerk commis principal *m*

series série *f*

service charge commission de service *f*

service counter guichet de service *m*

servicing a loan service d'un emprunt *m*

to **set the price** dégager le prix

to **set the rate of** tarifer

setting of rates tarification *f*

to **settle an account** régler un compte

settlement règlement *m*; *at settlement* au règlement

settlement account compte de règlement *m*

settlement and delivery system système de règlement livraison *m*

settlement date date de règlement *f*, date de liquidation *f*

settlement day jour de liquidation *m*

settlement of trades liquidation des opérations *f*

settlement period délai de règlement *m*, terme de liquidation *m*

settlement price cours de règlement *m*, cours de compensation *m*

settlement system système de règlements *m*

settlement value valeur liquidative *f*, valeur transactionnelle *f*

share action *f*; *to have shares in a company* détenir des actions d'une société; *to hold 5% of the shares in* détenir 5% du capital de

share account compte-titres *m*

share capital capital social *m*

share certificate certificat d'actions *m*, certificat titres *m*

share custody institution établissement dépositaire de titres *m*

share deal opération sur titre *f*

share dealing négoce de titres *m*, opérations de Bourse *fpl*

share delivery livraison de titres *f*

share dividend dividende d'action *m*

shareholder actionnaire *mf*, détenteur de titres *m*

shareholders actionnariat *m*, actionnaires *mpl*

shareholders' meeting assemblée des actionnaires *f*

shareholding [*stake*] participation *f*; [*ownership of shares*] actionnariat *m*; *to have a 5% shareholding in* détenir 5% du capital de

shareholding bank banquier actionnaire *m*

share index indice actions *m*, indice boursier *m*

share investment placement en actions *m*

share issue émission d'actions *f*, émission boursière *f*

share market marché des valeurs mobilières *m*, marché actions *m*

share movements mouvement des valeurs *m*

share option option sur actions *f*

share owner possesseur de valeurs *m*

share ownership actionnariat *m*

share portfolio portefeuille d'actions *m*, portefeuille-titres *m*

share price cours d'action *m*

share price index indice des cours d'actions *m*

share register registre des actions *m*

share split division d'actions *f*, fractionnement *m*

share subscription form bulletin de souscription d'actions *m*

share warrant bon de souscription d'actions *m*

share without voting rights certificat d'investissement *m*

shares quoted on the monthly settlement market valeurs admises au règlement mensuel *fpl*

sharp drop in prices chute brutale des cours *f*

sharp fall chute brutale *f*

sharp rise forte hausse *f*

sheet [*of bank statement, etc.*] feuillet *m*

shell centre centre boîte aux lettres *m*

short traite à courte échéance *f*, effet à courte échéance *m*

short *adj* court; *to be short* [*on Stock Exchange*] jouer à la baisse; *to go short* prendre une position courte; *to sell short* vendre à découvert; *to have a short position* être en position courte

short-dated bill traite à courte échéance *f*

short-dated security titre à courte échéance *m*

short maturity échéance proche *f*

short position position vendeur *f*

short rate taux court *m*

short sale vente à découvert *f*

short term court terme *m*

short-term *adj* à court terme; *to invest short-term* investir à court terme

short-term advances crédit de trésorerie *m*

short-term borrowings emprunts à court terme *mpl*

short-term credit crédit (à) court terme *m*

short-term deposits dépôts à court terme *mpl*

short-term financing financement à court terme *m*

short-term investment placement à court terme *m*

short-term loan prêt à court terme *m*

short-term money rate taux court monétaire *m*

short-term paper titres à courte échéance *mpl*

short-term rate taux à court terme *m*, taux court *m*

to **show a profit** dégager un bénéfice

to **shrink** se rétracter

shrinking contraction *f*

SIB (= Securities and Investments Board) ≈ COB *f*

sight: at sight à vue

sight bank deposit dépôt à vue *m*

sight bill effet à vue *m*

sight deposit dépôt à vue *m*

sight draft traite à vue *f*

sight maturity échéance à vue *f*

sight paper papier à vue *m*

to **sign** signer

signature signature *f*

signing of a contract conclusion d'un contrat *f*

silver argent *m*

simple credit prêt simple *m*

simple interest intérêt simple *m*

simple position position élémentaire *f*

simultaneous resale revente simultanée *f*

single currency monnaie unique *f*

single market marché unique *m*

size of a loan importance d'un crédit *f*

S&L (= Savings and Loan association) *Am* caisse d'épargne-logement *f*

slack [*market*] inactif

sliding scale échelle mobile *f*

slight fall in bond prices velléités de baisse des taux obligataires *fpl*

slight firming (of prices) hausse limitée (des cours) *f*

slight rise hausse de faible amplitude *f*

slight weakening (in prices) légère baisse (des cours) *f*

sluggish [*market*] inanimé, atone

slump affaissement *m*

small investor petit porteur *m*

small price movements faibles variations de cours *fpl*

smart card carte à puce *f*, carte à mémoire *f*

SO (= Standing Order) ordre de prélèvement permanent *m*, virement automatique *m*

to **soar** monter en flèche

soft loan prêt bonifié *m*

softs matières premières agricoles *fpl*

solicitation démarchage *m*

solvency ratio ratio de solvabilité *m*

sort(ing) code code banque et code guichet *m*

source of finance source de financement *f*

sovereign risk risque souverain *m*

special drawing right droit de tirage spécial *m*

specialized savings account compte d'épargne à régime spécial *m*

to **speculate** spéculer, jouer en Bourse

speculation spéculation *f*

speculation on the foreign exchange market spéculation sur les changes *f*

speculative spéculatif

speculative security valeur de spéculation *f*, valeur spéculative *f*

speculative value valeur de spéculation *f*

speculator spéculateur *m*

to **spend** dépenser

to **split shares** fractionner des actions

spot comptant *m*

spot credit crédit ponctuel *m*

spot market marché au comptant *m*

spot price cours au comptant *m*, cours spot *m*

spot quotation cotation à vue *f*

spot trading négociations au comptant *fpl*

spot transaction transaction au comptant *f*

spread [*on Stock Market*] opération mixte *f*, spread *m*; [*variance*] écart *m*

to **spread (out) over several financial years** étaler sur plusieurs exercices

spread of investments diversification des placements *f*

spread risk risque de spread *m*

spreading étalement *m*

spreadsheet feuille de calcul *f*; [*software*] tableur *m*

Square Mile: the Square Mile la City

squawkbox interphone reliant une salle de marchés à un courtier *m*

squeeze on margins écrasement des marges *m*

squeezing of margins laminage de marges *m*

stability stabilité *f*

stable stable

stag personne achetant des actions nouvellement émises *f*

to **stagger payments** échelonner des paiements

staggered payments versements échelonnés *mpl*

stake participation *f*

to **stamp a bill** viser un effet

stamp duty droits de timbre *mpl*

to **stand guarantor for** se porter garant envers

to **stand surety for** se porter caution pour qn, cautionner

Standard and Poors index indice S&P *m*

standard deviation écart type *m*

standardization normalisation *f*

standby credit facilities crédit standby *m*

standing order ordre de prélèvement permanent *m*, virement automatique *m*

standing order mandate autorisation de prélèvement permanent *f*

standstill atermoiement *m*

standstill agreement accord d'atermoiement *m*

start-up capital capital de départ *m*, capital initial *m*

State-chartered bank banque d'État *f*

State investment capital capital-investissement d'État *m*

state of the market état du marché *m*; [*Stock Market*] tenue de la Bourse *f*

statement affirmation *f*; [*document*] relevé *m*

statement of account relevé de compte *m*

statement of claim affirmation de créance *f*

status enquiry [*for credit*] renseignements de crédit *mpl*

statutory rate taux réglementé *m*, TR *m*

statutory reserves réserves statutaires *fpl*

steadiness of the market fermeté du marché *f*, fermeté des cours *f*

step-up bond obligation à taux progressif *f*

step-up rate loan crédit à taux progressif *m*

sterling livre sterling *f*, sterling *m*

sterling account compte en livres sterling *m*

sterling area zone sterling *f*

sterling traveller's cheque chèque de voyage en livres sterling *m*

stochastic stochastique

stock *Am* actions *fpl*, titres *mpl*

stockbroker agent de change *m*

Stock Exchange Bourse *f*, Bourse des valeurs *f*

Stock Exchange *adj* boursier

Stock Exchange circles milieux boursiers *mpl*

Stock Exchange close clôture de la Bourse *f*

Stock Exchange commitments engagements à la Bourse *mpl*

Stock Exchange crash krach boursier *m*

Stock Exchange journal journal de la Bourse *m*

Stock Exchange order ordre de Bourse *m*

Stock Exchange transactions transactions boursières *fpl*

stock index indice boursier *m*

stockjobber teneur de marché *m*

Stock Market Bourse *f*, marché boursier *m*

Stock Market *adj* boursier

Stock Market crash krach boursier *m*

Stock Market crisis crise boursière *f*

Stock Market cycle cycle boursier *m*

Stock Market gamble jeu de Bourse *m*

Stock Market index indice boursier *m*

Stock Market jargon langage boursier *m*

Stock Market movement mouvement boursier *m*

Stock Market panic panique boursière *f*

Stock Market price cours de la Bourse *m*

Stock Market rise hausse des cours *f*

Stock Market transaction opération de Bourse *f*

Stock Market trend orientation de la Bourse *f*

Stock Market value valeur en Bourse *f*

stock-option programme plan de stock-options *m*

to **stop a cheque** faire opposition à un chèque

to **stop payments** suspendre les paiements

stop-limit order ordre stop à cours limité *m*

stop loss limit stop loss *m*

stop order ordre stop *m*

stoppage of payment(s) arrêt de paiement *m*

stopped [*payment, cheque*] en opposition

stopping of a payment suspension d'un paiement *f*

store card carte privative *f*

straddle stellage *m*

straight bond obligation classique *f*

straightline depreciation amortissement linéaire *m*

to **strike a deal** conclure un marché

strike price prix de levée *m*

stripped démembré

stripped bond obligation démembrée *f*

stripping démembrement *m*

strong currency monnaie forte *f*

structural risk risque de structure *m*

stub [*of cheque*] talon *m*

student loan prêt étudiant *m*

subject offer offre de vente sans engagement *f*

subject to collection sauf bonne fin, SBF

subject to payment moyennant paiement

subordinated debt dettes subordonnées *fpl*

sub-participation sous-participation *f*

to **subscribe** souscrire

to **subscribe for shares** souscrire à des actions

subscribed capital capital souscrit *m*

subscription souscription *f*

subscription period période de souscription *f*

subsidization bonification *f*

subsidized loan prêt conventionné *m*

subtotal sous-total *m*

to **subtract** soustraire

sum somme *f*

sum payable charge à payer *f*

summary balance sheet bilan condensé *m*

summons to pay commandement à payer *m*

super-NOW dépôt à terme mobilisable à rémunération libre *m*

supplementary income revenus complémentaires *mpl*

supplier credit crédit-fournisseur *m*

to **supply funds** céder des fonds

to **support a currency** soutenir le cours d'une monnaie
surety caution *f*; *to stand surety for* être caution personnelle de; *as surety* en caution
surety for a loan sûreté en garantie d'une créance *f*
surplus surplus *m*
survivor's pension pension de réversion *f*
to **suspend payment** suspendre les paiements
suspense account compte d'attente *m*
swap swap *m*, échange financier *m*
to **swap** swapper, swaper
swap rate taux swap *m*

SWIFT (= Society for Worldwide Interbank Financial Telecommunication) Swift
SWIFT transfer virement SWIFT *m*
to **swing** osciller
swing line crédit de sécurité *m*
to **swipe** [*credit card*] passer au lecteur de cartes
Switch Switch *m*
switching arbitrage *m*
syndicate syndicat *m*
to **syndicate** [*lending*] syndiquer
syndicated loan crédit consortial *m*, prêt en participation *m*
syndication syndication *f*

T

to **take a position** prendre une position
to **take deposits** collecter des dépôts
to **take one's profit** prendre son gain
to **take on a risk** assumer un risque
to **take out a lease on** prendre à bail
to **take out a loan** contracter un crédit, souscrire un prêt
to **take out a mortgage on** prendre un crédit immobilier pour

takeover prise de contrôle *f*, rachat *m*
takeover bid OPA *f*, offre publique d'achat *f*; *to be the subject of a takeover bid* être l'objet d'une OPA; *ripe for takeover* opéable
takeover bid for shares offre publique d'échange *f*, OPE *f*
takeover fever opeamania *f*
taker for a put and call donneur d'option *m*

taker of an option optant *m*

taking delivery of shares levée des titres *f*

tangible asset actif corporel *m*

tangible fixed asset immobilisation corporelle *f*

to **tap funds** drainer des fonds, ponctionner des fonds

tapering rate taux dégressif *m*

target company entreprise cible *f*

tariff tarif *m*

tariff *adj* tarifaire

tax impôt *m*

tax authorities fisc *m*

tax credit avoir fiscal *m*

tax deduction at source perception à la source *f*

tax domicile foyer fiscal *m*

Tax Exempt Special Savings Account plan d'épargne exempt d'impôts *m*

tax-free exempt d'impôts

tax haven paradis fiscal *m*

tax impact incidences fiscales *fpl*

tax loophole échappatoire fiscal *m*

tax man fisc *m*

tax return déclaration fiscale *f*

tax specialist fiscaliste *mf*

taxable income revenu imposable *m*

telephone banking service de banque par téléphone *m*

telex transfer virement par télex *m*

teller guichetier *m*

term [*duration*] durée *f*; [*condition*] terme *m*

term deposit dépôt à terme *m*

term loan prêt à échéance fixe *m*

term of loan durée de crédit *f*

terms (and conditions) of payment conditions de paiement *fpl*

to **terminate a contract** dénoncer un contrat

termination clause clause de résiliation *f*

TESSA (= Tax Exempt Special Savings Account) plan d'épargne exempt d'impôts *m*

theta thêta *m*

thin margin marge faible *f*

third party security garantie de tiers *f*

thousand millier *m*

thousand francs kilofranc *m*

thousand million milliard *m*

three-month money argent à trois mois *m*

three-month PIBOR PIBOR 3 mois *m*

thrifts *Am* caisses d'épargne *fpl*

through-the-wall automated teller machine distributeur automatique de billets *m*

to **thwart speculation** contrecarrer les mouvements speculatifs

tick (size) échelon de cotation *m*

ticker (tape) téléscripteur *m*

to **tie up** [*funds*] immobiliser

tied up capital immobilisation de capitaux *f*

time bill traite à date fixe *f*

time deposit dépôt à terme *m*

time factor facteur temps *m*

time spread spread calendaire *m*

time value valeur temporelle *f*

timing difference décalage temporel *m*

tin étain *m*, fer-blanc *m*

title deed titre de propriété *m*, acte de propriété *m*

tontine tontine *f*

tontine *adj* tontinier

total montant total *m*

to **total** [*add up*] totaliser; [*add up to*] se chiffrer à

total amount montant total *m*

total lending encours *m*

totalling chiffrage *m*

totally: *to totally close (out) a position* clore une position en totalité

town bill effet sur place *m*

tradable securities titres négociables *mpl*

to **trade** commercer; [*on Stock Market*] négocier

trade credit crédit commercial *m*

trade debtor compte client *m*, créance client *f*

trade discounting escompte commercial *m*

trade price [*on Stock Market*] prix de négociation *m*

trade receivables crédit de mobilisation de créances commerciales *m*

tradeable négociable

tradeable certificates of deposit certificats de dépôts négociables *mpl*

traded option option négociable *f*

traded options market marché d'options négociables *m*

traded securities market marché de titres négociables *m*

trader opérateur *m*, trader *m*, négociateur *m*

trading négociation *f*; *trading in X was suspended* la cotation des actions X était suspendue

trading day jour de Bourse *m*, Bourse *f*

trading fees frais de négociation *mpl*

trading floor corbeille *f*, parquet *m*

trading hours [*on Stock Exchange*] horaires criés *mpl*, heures d'ouverture *fpl*

trading instrument outil de spéculation *m*

trading member intermédiaire négociateur *m*

trading month mois d'échéance *m*

trading order ordre de négociation *m*

trading session séance boursière *f*

trading system système de place *m*

traditional option option classique *f*

tranche tranche *f*

to **transact banking business** traiter des opérations de banque

transaction transaction *f*, opération *f*

transaction charge commission de mouvement *f*

transaction cost coût de transaction *m*

transaction costs frais de transaction *mpl*

transaction cum rights opération sans détachement de droit *f*

transaction date date d'opération *f*

transaction note avis d'opération *m*

transaction tax impôt de Bourse *m*

transaction volume volume des transactions *m*

transfer transfert *m*; [*of assets*] cession *f*; [*of funds*] virement *m*

to **transfer** transférer; [*assets*] céder; [*funds*] virer

to **transfer an amount from one account to another** reverser une somme d'un compte sur un autre

transfer advice avis de virement *m*

transfer by endorsement transmission par endossement *f*

transfer capital capital transmission *m*

transfer cheque chèque de virement *m*

transfer of capital transfert de capitaux *m*

transfer of funds transfert de fonds *m*

transfer of shares transfert d'actions *m*

transfer order ordre de virement *m*

transfer risk risque de transfert *m*

transferable transférable; [*assets*] cessible

transferable by endorsement transmissible par endossement

transferee cessionnaire *mf*

transfers department service des transferts *m*

to **transport by armed guard** convoyer

traveller's cheque chèque de voyage *m*

treasurer trésorier *m*

Treasury Trésor *m*, ministère de l'Économie et des Finances *m*

Treasury bill bon du Trésor *m*

Treasury bond bon du Trésor *m*

Treasury Department Trésor public *m*; [*in bank*] service de trésorerie *m*, trésorerie *f*

Treasury note bon du Trésor *m*

treasury swap échange cambiste *m*

trial balance balance de vérification *f*

triple-A rated noté triple "A"

triple-A rating notation triple "A" *f*

truncation [*dematerialization*] troncation *f*

trust fidéicommis *m*; *to hold in trust* tenir par fidéicommis

trust bank banque de gestion de patrimoine *f*

trustee fiduciaire *mf*

trust(ee) account compte en fidéicommis *m*

trustee department service fiduciaire *m*

tune: to the tune of à hauteur de

turnaround period délai aller-retour *m*

turnover chiffre d'affaires *m*, CA *m*

two-speed monetary union union monétaire à deux vitesses *f*

U

UCITS (= Undertaking for Collective Investment in Transferable Securities) OPCVM *m*

uncalled capital capital non appelé *m*

uncleared cheque chèque non crédité *m*

uncoupling décrochage *m*

uncovered cheque chèque sans provision *m*

uncovered position position non couverte *f*, découvert boursier *m*

uncovered short position position courte non couverte *f*

underlying asset actif sous-jacent *m*, actif support *m*

underlying bond support obligataire *m*

underlying option option fille *f*

to **underwrite** souscrire

to **underwrite a bond issue** garantir un emprunt

underwriter garant *m*

underwriting garantie d'émission *f*

underwriting fee commission de garantie *f*

underwriting syndicate syndicat de bonne fin *m*, syndicat d'émission *m*, syndicat de prise ferme *m*

undiluted [*earnings*] non dilué

undischarged bankrupt failli non réhabilité *m*

undiscountable inescomptable

unexpected rise in prices hausse inopinée des cours *f*

to **unfreeze credits** dégeler des crédits

uniform rate taux uniforme *m*

unit capitalization capitalisation unitaire *f*

unit holder détenteur d'unité *m*

unit of account unité de compte *f*

unit of the underlying

instrument unité de l'action sous-jacente *f*

unit trust société d'investissement à capital variable *f*, SICAV *f*, OPCVM *m*

Unitime Unitime *m*

universal bank banque universelle *f*

unlimited profit gain illimité *m*

unlimited risk risque illimité *m*

unlisted non-admis à la cote; [*share*] incoté

unlisted market marché hors cote *m*, Bourse coulisse *f*

unlisted securities valeurs du second marché *fpl*

unlisted securities market second marché *m*

unlisted security valeur non cotée *f*

unpaid bill impayé *m*

unpaid debt créance impayée *f*

unpaid-up share action non libérée *f*

unquoted incoté, non-inscrit à la cote

unrealized loss perte latente *f*

unsecured loan prêt non garanti *m*

unsettled [*market*] instable

unsteadiness of prices instabilité des cours *f*

unsteady [*market*] irrégulier, instable; *to be unsteady* [*currency*] vaciller

untrad(e)able incotable

to **unwind one's positions** se dégager de ses positions

up by en hausse de

update actualisation *f*

to **update** actualiser

upper limit borne haute *f*

upper price limit prix plafond *m*

upside risk risque de hausse *m*

upward movement mouvement
  ascensionnel *m*
upward trend tendance
  haussière *f*

US dollar dollar américain *m*
**USM (= Unlisted Securities
  Market)** second marché *m*
usury rate taux de l'usure *m*

vagaries of the market jeu du
  marché *m*
valid valable
to **validate** valider
validity date date de validité *f*
valuation valorisation *f*
value valeur *f*; *when will I have
  value?* [*after lodging funds*]
  quelle sera la date de valeur?
to **value** valoriser, évaluer
value-added tax taxe à la valeur
  ajoutée *f*
value date date de valeur *f*, jour de
  valeur *m*
value for collection valeur à
  l'encaissement *f*
value today valeur ce jour *f*
value today trade transaction
  valeur jour *f*
vanilla swap swap vanilla *m*
variable variable *f*
variable monetary rate taux
  variable monétaire *m*
variable rate taux variable *m*

variable-rate à taux variable, à
  revenu variable
variable-rate interest intérêt
  variable *m*
variable-rate mortgage prêt
  hypothécaire à taux variable *m*
variable-rate security valeur à
  revenu variable *f*
variable-yield à revenu variable
variable-yield security effet à
  rendement variable *m*
variation margin marge *f*
VAT (= Value-Added Tax) TVA *f*
vaults salle des coffres-forts *f*
vector vecteur *m*
vega vega *m*
venture capital capital-risque *m*
venture capital company société
  de capital-risque *f*
venture capitalist pourvoyeur de
  capital-risque *m*
vertical spread écart vertical *m*
very short-term à très court terme
very short-term loan crédit à très

court terme *m*
Visa® carte Visa® *f*, Carte
  Bleue® *f*
volatile volatil
volatility volatilité *f*
volatility assumptions hypothèses

de volatilité *fpl*
volume of trading volume de
  transactions *m*
vostro account compte vostre *m*,
  compte loro *m*
voucher bon *m*

warrant [*for shares*] warrant *m*,
  bon de souscription *m*
wash trading opérations
  fictives *fpl*
to **weaken** [*market prices*] faiblir
weakening of a currency
  fragilisation d'une monnaie *f*
wealth richesse *f*
weekly return situation
  hebdomadaire *f*
to **weight an average** pondérer
  une moyenne
weighting pondération *f*
white knight chevalier blanc *m*
wholesale bank banque de gros *f*
wholesale banking banque de
  gros *f*
wholesale deposit gros dépôt *m*
wholesale market marché de gré à
  gré entre banques *m*
wicket *Am* guichet *m*
to **wind up** [*company*]
  dissoudre

winding up of a company
  dissolution d'une société *f*
window [*in bank*] guichet *m*
to **window-dress the accounts**
  camoufler le bilan
wire transfer virement bancaire
  télégraphique *m*
to **withdraw** [*money*] retirer
to **withdraw from circulation**
  [*coin*] démonétiser, retirer de la
  circulation
withdrawal retrait *m*
withdrawal from circulation
  démonétisation *f*
withdrawal limit plafond de
  retrait *m*
withdrawal slip bordereau de
  remboursement *m*
to **withhold** prélever
working capital fonds de
  roulement *m*, capital de
  roulement *m*
working capital facilities crédit

de restructuration de fonds de
roulement *m*
working capital requirements
besoin en fonds de roulement *m*,
BFR *m*
working day jour ouvrable *m*, jour
ouvré *m*
World Bank Banque Mondiale *f*
world banking industry industrie
bancaire mondiale *f*
worth: to be worth valoir
worthless amount non-valeur *f*
to **write a cheque** créer un

chèque
to **write off** amortir
to **write off a bad debt** défalquer
une mauvaise créance
to **write out a cheque** émettre un
chèque
writedown dépréciation *f*
write-off of expenditure
amortissement-dépenses *m*
writer of an option émetteur
d'une option *m*
written advice préavis écrit *m*

YZ

year: *10-year government bond*
emprunt d'État à dix ans *m*; *per
year* par an
year-end closing of accounts
clôture annuelle des livres *f*
year-on-year increase hausse sur
un an *f*
year-on-year rate taux annuel
glissant *m*
to **yield** rendre; *to make sth yield a
profit* faire fructifier qch
to **yield annually** rapporter par an

to **yield interest** porter intérêt,
rapporter des intérêts
yield curve courbe de rendement *f*,
courbe des taux *f*
yield to redemption taux de
rendement actuariel *m*, taux
actuariel *m*
zero-coupon bond obligation à
zéro coupon *f*
zero-coupon strip titre de dette
synthétique sans coupon *m*
zinc zinc *m*

Annexes
Appendices

TRAITE BANCAIRE
BANK DRAFT – FRANCE

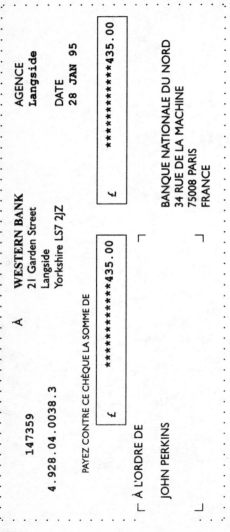

147359

4.928.04.0038.3

À   **WESTERN BANK**
21 Garden Street
Langside
Yorkshire LS7 2JZ

AGENCE
Langside

DATE
28 **JAN 95**

PAYEZ CONTRE CE CHÈQUE LA SOMME DE

£   ************435.00

£   ************435.00

À L'ORDRE DE

JOHN PERKINS

BANQUE NATIONALE DU NORD
34 RUE DE LA MACHINE
75008 PARIS
FRANCE

TRAITE BANCAIRE
BANK DRAFT – UK

WESTERN BANK

International Operations, PO Box 635
37 Station Road, Ulverton, Manchester M89 2SY

Draft Number DFT13983S927S987
Date   Sixteenth January 1995

FRF***,***,875-45

or order

Pay against this cheque to   MARIE-CLAUDE BOUCHER

The Sum of

FRENCH FRANCS Eight Hundred Seventy Five.45/100***

Per pro Western Bank PLC

To   BANQUE NATIONALE DU NORD
21 rue de Tourcoing
62900 Calais
FRANCE

Debit our account No: 00487286

REMISE DE CHÈQUES (FRANCE)
BANK GIRO CREDIT SLIP (FRANCE)

BANQUE NATIONALE DU NORD

REMISE DE CHÈQUES

NOM DU BÉNÉFICIAIRE

NOM DE L'AGENCE QUI TIENT LE COMPTE

code

numéro de compte

0

agence de remise (si différente de l'agence qui tient le compte)

référence

visa de la Banque Nationale du Nord

date et signature du client

établissement payeur — nom du tireur

montant

F

F

montant total

nombre de chèques

hors département

sur département

pour plus de 8 chèques, veuillez indiquer seulement le total et joindre un relevé séparé des chèques remis

n'oubliez pas de signer vos chèques

REÇU DE VOTRE REMISE – CONSERVEZ-LE – NE LE TRANSMETTEZ PAS À VOTRE AGENCE

REMISE DE CHÈQUES (ROYAUME-UNI)
BANK GIRO CREDIT SLIP (UK)

(Recto)

(Verso)

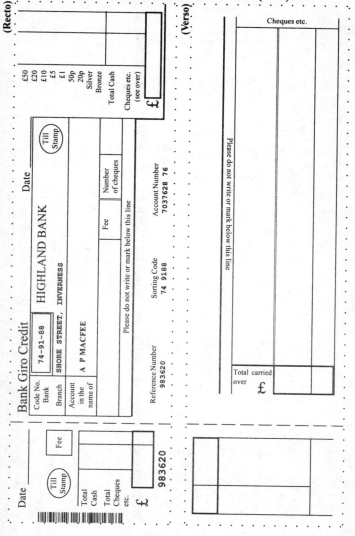

£50
£20
£10
£5
£1
50p
20p
Silver
Bronze

Total Cash

Cheques etc. (see over)

£

Till Stamp

HIGHLAND BANK

SHORE STREET, INVERNESS

Date

Bank Giro Credit

Code No. / Bank   74-91-88

Branch

Account in the name of   A P MACFEE

Fee   Number of cheques

Please do not write or mark below this line

Reference Number
983620

Sorting Code
74 9188

Account Number
7037628 76

Cheques etc.

Please do not write or mark below this line

Total carried over
£

Date

Till Stamp

Fee

Total Cash
Total Cheques etc.

£

983620

173

CHÈQUE ET REPORT D'OPÉRATIONS
CHEQUE AND RECORD OF ENTRIES

DATE _____ ORDRE _____

OBJET _____

SÉRIE 76   N° CHÈQUE 2987345   ANCIEN SOLDE _____   MONTANT _____   NOUVEAU SOLDE _____

CRÉDIT INDUSTRIEL   CAISSE RÉGIONALE DE CRÉDIT INDUSTRIEL MUTUEL   B.P.F. [   ]

80 av de la Libération - 37645 Chinon-le-Gué

PAYEZ CONTRE CE CHÈQUE **NON ENDOSSABLE SAUF**
AU PROFIT D'UNE BANQUE, CAISSE D'ÉPARGNE, OU ÉTABLISSEMENT ASSIMILÉ _____

À _____

_____ LE _____ 19 __

COMPENSABLE À
CHINON-GARE

PAYABLE À
CHINON-GARE
43983746

NANTAIS MARIE-CLAUDE
73 RUE DES VIGNERONS
37921 ST MARTIN-SUR-LOIRE

N° Compte 33830291 6000
N° Chèque 2984750 Série 83

• 2984750 • 03087435 6008   03383746000

Date	Libellé	Débit	Crédit	SOLDE	Date	Libellé	Débit	Crédit	SOLDE	Date	Libellé	Débit	Crédit	SOLDE

CHÈQUE ET REPORT D'OPÉRATIONS
CHEQUE AND RECORD OF ENTRIES

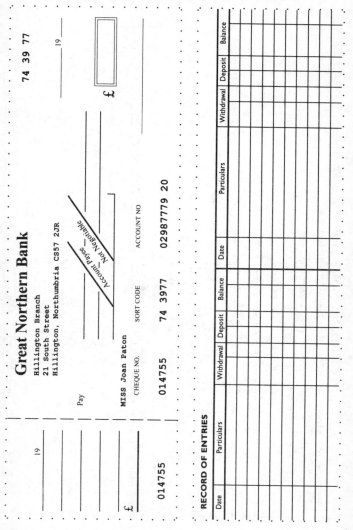

Great Northern Bank

Hillington Branch
21 South Street
Hillington, Northumbria CS57 2TR

74 39 77

19____

£

Pay _____

Account Payee — Not Negotiable

MISS Joan Paton

CHEQUE NO.   SORT CODE   ACCOUNT NO

014755   74 3977   02987779 20

19____

£

014755

RECORD OF ENTRIES

Date	Particulars	Withdrawal	Deposit	Balance	Date	Particulars	Withdrawal	Deposit	Balance

175

AUTORISATION DE PRÉLÈVEMENT (FRANCE)
DIRECT DEBIT INSTRUCTION (FRANCE)

AUTORISATION DE PRÉLÈVEMENT

J'autorise l'établissement teneur de mon compte à effectuer sur ce dernier les prélèvements ordonnés par France Télécom.

Je pourrai en faire suspendre l'exécution par simple demande à l'établissement teneur de mon compte, ou par simple lettre adressée à France Télécom.

Numéro(s) d'appel téléphonique(s) ou télex

LE TITULAIRE DU COMPTE À DÉBITER

COMPTE À DÉBITER

| Établissement | Codes Guichet | Numéro de compte | Clé RIB |

Portez les informations indiquées sur votre Relevé d'Identité Bancaire (R.I.B.), Postal (R.I.P.) ou Caisse d'Épargne (R.I.C.E.).

DATE   SIGNATURE

N° NATIONAL D'ÉMETTEUR
002305

À retourner à :
France Télécom
77451 MARNE-LA-VALLÉE CEDEX 2

NOM ET ADDRESSE DE L'ÉTABLISSEMENT TENEUR DU COMPTE À DÉBITER (votre banque ou C.C.P. ou Caisse d'Épargne)

N°   RUE
CODE POSTAL   VILLE

N'oubliez pas de joindre un R.I.P. ou un R.I.B.

Les informations contenues dans la présente demande ne seront utilisées que pour les seules nécessités de la gestion et pourront donner lieu à un exercice du droit individuel d'accès auprès du créancier à l'adresse ci-dessus, dans les conditions prévues par la délibération n° 80 du 01/04/80 de la Commission Nationale de l'Informatique et des Libertés.

AUTORISATION DE PRÉLÈVEMENT (ROYAUME UNI)
DIRECT DEBIT INSTRUCTION (UK)

INSTRUCTION TO YOUR BANK/BUILDING SOCIETY TO PAY DIRECT DEBITS.

Please complete parts 1-5 to instruct your branch to make payments from your account.
Then return to: STRATHCLYDE REGIONAL COUNCIL at the address shown in your Demand Notice.

Rates Reference:

Originator's Identification Number.
(For office use only)

1. Full postal address of your branch

   To: The Manager

   _____ Bank/Bldg.Soc.

   Address _____

   _____ Postcode

2. Name(s) of account holder

3. Bank/Building Society account number.

4. Branch sort code.

   Banks/Building Societies may refuse to accept instructions to pay direct debits from some types of account.

5. Instruction to your Bank/Building Society.

   Please pay Strathclyde Regional Council Direct Debits from the account detailed on this instruction subject to the safeguards assured by the Direct Debit Guarantee.

   Signatures of Account Holders

   Signature(s) _____

   Address _____

   Date _____

RELEVÉ DE COMPTE (FRANCE)
BANK STATEMENT (FRANCE)

(Recto)

EXTRAIT No 01-005

CRÉDIT INDUSTRIEL DU CENTRE

DESTINATAIRE POSTAL ....

{
1F84628508846280
MARIE-CLAUDE NANTAIS
73 RUE DES VIGNERONS
37921 ST MARTIN-SUR-LOIRE
}

TITULAIRE

MLLE   NANTAIS MARIE-CLAUDE

	ANCIEN SOLDE AU 03/04/95	NOUVEAU SOLDE AU 02/05/95
DÉPOT À VUE 32558407779	1546,55	2023,55

(Verso)

EXTRAIT No 01-005

CRÉDIT INDUSTRIEL DU CENTRE

Période du 03/04/95 au 02/05/95

AGENCE : CHINON-GARE   MLLE

TEL : 36-72-88-00   NANTAIS MARIE-CLAUDE

DATE TRAITEMENT J M	LIBELLÉ	DATE VALEUR J M	VOS DÉBITS	VOS CRÉDITS	SOLDES	Déb
	DEPOT A VUE					
	No 32558407779	votre ancien	solde au	03/01/95	1546,55	
20 4	REM 1 CHÈQUE	21 4		375,00	2398,55	
24 4	REM 1 CHÈQUE	25 4		477,00	2023,55	
	CUMUL			852,00		
		votre nouveau	solde au	04/07/95	2398,55	

RELEVÉ DE COMPTE (ROYAUME-UNI)
BANK STATEMENT (UK)

Western Bank

STATEMENT OF ACCOUNT

37 Station Road
Ulverton
MANCHESTER M89 2SY

Branch Code	62-74-00
Account No.	00474028
Date	09 JUN95
Page No.	036

7400   1038476/01/02

MISS ID SMITH
48 STEVENSON STREET
Ulverton
MANCHESTER M89 4TZ

Date	Description	Withdrawals	Pay-ins	Balance (DR = Overdrawn)
1995	BALANCE BROUGHT FORWARD			25.98DR
10MAY	010375		59.99	34.01
19MAY	INTER A/C TRANSFER		200	234.01
26MAY	YG7523 MAY26 13.44 ROYAL BANK	40.00	194.01	
30MAY	SALARY		804.55	998.56
1JUN	MORTGAGE PAYMENT 9282938461984	206.55		792.01

Total Withdrawals	£246.55
Total Pay-ins	£1258.55
Overdraft Limit	£100.00

Where debtor interest is applied details of the rate(s) used and a clear explanation of the manner of calculation are available on request.

Demande d'ouverture de crédit documentaire

BANQUE NATIONALE DU NORD
DEMANDE D'OUVERTURE DE CRÉDIT DOCUMENTAIRE

Nom et adresse du donneur d'ordre

				BANQUE NATIONALE DU NORD
Compte n°	Guichet	Cte Gal	Cte individuel	Guichet : ....

Suivant instructions ci-dessous et lignes marquées d'une croix, veuillez ouvrir pour notre compte un crédit documentaire :

- [ ] **révocable** (pouvant être modifié ou annulé à tout moment) sans responsabilité de votre part ni de la part de votre correspondant
- [ ] **irrévocable**, c'est-à-dire irrévocable de votre part, à faire notifier par votre correspondant sans qu'il y ajoute sa confirmation
- [ ] **irrévocable et confirmé**, c'est-à-dire irrévocable de votre part et de celle de votre correspondant qui, en confirmant le crédit, ajoutera son propre engagement au vôtre
- [ ] **transférable**   [ ] **non transférable**

chez

- [ ] votre correspondant

par
- [ ] lettre recommandée
- [ ] lettre ordinaire
- [ ] lettre avion
- [ ] télégramme de nuit (1/2 tarif)
- [ ] télégramme ordinaire   Telex [ ] succinct [ ] détaillé

en faveur de

validité

Date :   Lieu :

montant

[ ] environ   [ ] maximum

---

réalisable

- [ ] à vue
- [ ] par acceptation par vous-même de traites à :   jours [ ] de vue   [ ] de la date d'expédition
- [ ] par acceptation par votre correspondant de traites à :   jours   des documents

expéditions partielles   transbordements   expédition de :
à :
- [ ] autorisées [ ] interdites   [ ] autorisés [ ] interdits   au plus tard le :

---

conditions d'expédition

- [ ] FOB
- [ ] CAF ou CIF
- [ ] C et F
- [ ] FAS
- [ ] départ d'usine
- [ ] franco sur wagon point de départ
- [ ] franco rendu point de destination
- [ ] franco frontière
- [ ] à préciser, ex. : franco frontière/franco frontière italienne

---

contre remise des documents suivants à nous adresser

- [ ] facture commerciale en .... exemplaires
- [ ] jeu complet de connaissements net de réserves à bord à ordre : ....
....
....
- [ ] duplicata de lettre de voiture internationale ferroviaire estampillé par la gare de départ *
- [ ] lettre de voiture internationale routière *
- [ ] lettre de transport aérien ....
  * établie au nom et à l'adresse de : ....
....
....
- [ ] notify ou consignes éventuelles

police ou certificat d'assurance couvrant les risques suivants : ....

- [ ] note de poids
- [ ] liste de colisage
- [ ] certificat sanitaire délivré le jour de l'embarquement

par :

- [ ] certificat d'origine
- [ ]
- [ ]
- [ ]

---

relatif à

nature des marchandises, quantité, prix, etc.

Les documents devront être présentés à votre correspondant dans les   jours de la date d'expédition.

- [ ] Assurance souscrite par nos soins. Délégation à votre profit.
- [ ] Assurance souscrite par le vendeur. Nous ne désirons cependant pas de document d'assurance.
- [ ] Marchandise non assurée.

T.S.V.P.

Copie à conserver
par le donneur d'ordre

180

THAMESIDE BANK

APPLICATION FOR DOCUMENTARY CREDIT

Choice indicated thus [X]   Date:

To Thameside Bank Branch: Sorting code:	40A	Please open irrevocable ☐ transferable ☐ revocable ☐ documentary credit Transmit by
59 Applicant:		☐ teletransmission ☐ airmail ☐ preadvise main details by teletransmission
50 Beneficiary:	**31D**	Expiry date:
	32B	Amount (currency, words and figures)
57 Beneficiary's Bank (if known)		The amount to be drawn in full unless one of the following choices is made:
	39	☐ up to ☐ about (+/-10%)
Credit available to beneficiary against presentation of documents ☐ at sight ☐ after days calculated from ☐ plus beneficiary's draft	**44**	Shipped: Dispatched: Taken in charge From To

71B   Charges for applicant's account:
 	
    ☐ all ☐ only Thameside Bank
    Charges for beneficiary's account:
 	
    ☐ all ☐ only other bank's
	43P	Part shipments allowed ☐ Yes ☐ No

	43T	Transhipments allowed ☐ Yes ☐ No*
	48	Presentation of documents must be made within days after date of issue of transport document but prior to expiry of the Credit.

45A   Description of goods:

46A   Documents required (other documents may be shown on separate sheet and attached hereto)

☐   Invoice in original and copies

☐ Air waybill: ☐   Freight forwarder's air waybill: ☐   Transport document: indicating goods taken in charge and consigned to:

marked ☐ freight payable at destination ☐ freight prepaid

☐ Marine bills of lading ☐ Combined transport* bills of lading consisting of full set, clean on board, issued to order,

blank endorsed and marked ☐ freight payable at destination ☐ freight prepaid; notify:

☐   Insurance policy or certificate in original and   copies endorsed in blank for the invoice value of the goods plus   % (minimum 10%) covering All Risks including War Risks, Strikes (together with Riots and Civil Commotions)

Further instructions:

*Before prohibiting transhipment, check that uninterrupted carriage is possible. Transhipment is inseparable from combined transport documents.

RELEVÉ D'IDENTITÉ BANCAIRE
BANK DETAILS FORM

(Ce document n'existe pas en GB et aux USA)

(Recto)

N° Premier Chèque		N° Dernier Chèque		F	RELEVÉ D'IDENTITÉ BANCAIRE

CRÉDIT INDUSTRIEL
CAISSE RÉGIONALE DU CRÉDIT
INDUSTRIEL MUTUEL
80 av de la Libération
37645 CHINON-LE-GUÉ

SIMPLIFIEZ-VOUS LA VIE
Utilisez les services de votre carte bancaire
Attention : ne conservez jamais votre code
secret avec votre carte

Code Étabt	Code Guichet	N° Compte	Clé R.I.B.	NOM ET ADRESSE DU TITULAIRE
19805	07800	83081699000	10	NANTAIS MARIE-CLAUDE

73 RUE DES VIGNERONS
37921 ST MARTIN-SUR-LOIRE

LIEU DE PAIEMENT
CHINON-GARE

(Verso)

RELEVÉ D'IDENTITÉ BANCAIRE
Remettez ce relevé à tout organisme
souhaitant connaître vos références
bancaires pour la domiciliation de
virements ou de prélèvements à votre
compte. Vous éviterez ainsi erreurs et
retards d'exécution.

RENOUVELLEMENT DE CHÉQUIER
- Les chéquiers comportent 33 chèques.
  La fabrication de votre prochain chéquier
  sera déclenchée automatiquement en
  fonction des formules utilisées.
- En cas d'expédition à domicile la
  tarification applicable est conforme aux
  conditions générales de banque.

ACCUSÉ RÉCEPTION DE CARNET DE CHÈQUES

Nous accusons réception du présent carnet de chèques dont les numéros figurent au verso en
date du _____

Nous dégageons la Caisse Régionale de toute responsabilité en cas de perte ou de sous-traction
desdits chèques.

Signature :

(à retourner dès réception du carnet).

POUVOIR POUR REMISE DE CARNET DE CHÈQUES

À M _____ à qui je donne pouvoir pour retirer ce carnet de chèques en mon nom.

À _____ le _____ Signature du Titulaire,   Signature du Mandataire.

MODES DE PAIEMENT
PAYMENT METHODS

Paiement traditionnel du commerçant par chèque
Traditional payment of a retailer by cheque

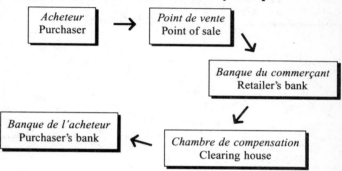

Paiement électronique du commerçant par carte
Electronic payment of a retailer by card

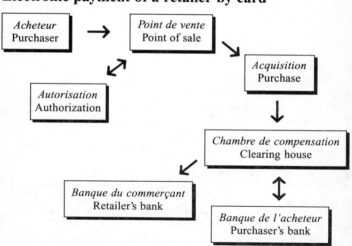

Exemple de circuit de la monnaie électronique
Example of electronic cashflow

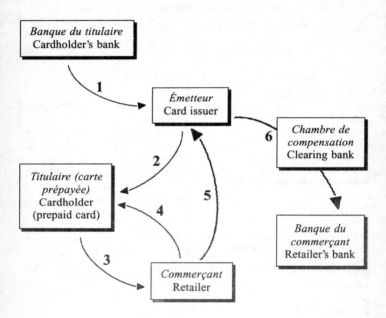

1   *Le titulaire de carte paye 100£ (liquide/chèque/transfert) pour sa carte*
    Cardholder pays £100 (cash/cheque/transfer) for card
2   *Émission ou réapprovisionnement de 100£ sur la carte*
    Issue or recharging of card with £100
3   *Paiement de 10£, créditées sur le compte du commerçant*
    Payment of £10; credit retailer with £10
4   *Les 10£ sont débitées de la carte (le solde restant sur la carte est donc de 90£)*
    Debit card with £10 (now £90 credit left on card)
5   *L'émetteur collecte électroniquement 10£ auprès du commerçant*
    Issuer collects £10 electronically from retailer
6   *Règlement de 10£ via une chambre de compensation envers la banque du commerçant*
    Settlement of £10 via clearing bank to the retailer's bank

MONNAIES

couronne *f* crown
deutschemark *m* deutschmark
dinar *m* dinar
dollar *m* dollar
dollar américain *m* US dollar,
  American dollar
dollar australien *m* Australian
  dollar
dollar canadien *m* Canadian
  dollar
dollar de Hong Kong *m* Hong
  Kong dollar
drachme *f* drachma
escudo *m* escudo
florin *m* guilder, florin
franc *m* franc
franc belge *m* Belgian franc
franc français *m* French franc
franc suisse *m* Swiss franc
lire *f* lira
livre *f* pound
livre irlandaise *f* punt
livre sterling *f* pound sterling
mark *m* mark
peseta *f* peseta
peso *m* peso
rand *m* rand
rial *m* rial
rouble *m* rouble
roupie *f* rupee
schilling *m* schilling
shilling *m* shilling
yen *m* yen

CURRENCIES

American dollar dollar américain *m*
Australian dollar dollar
  australien *m*
Belgian franc franc belge *m*
Canadian dollar dollar canadien *m*
crown couronne *f*
deutschmark deutschemark *m*
dinar dinar *m*
dollar dollar *m*
drachma drachme *f*
escudo escudo *m*
florin florin *m*
franc franc *m*
French franc franc français *m*
guilder florin *m*
Hong Kong dollar dollar de Hong
  Kong *m*
lira lire *f*
mark mark *m*
peseta peseta *f*
peso peso *m*
pound livre *f*
pound sterling livre sterling *f*
punt livre irlandaise *f*
rand rand *m*
rial rial *m*
rouble rouble *m*
rupee roupie *f*
schilling schilling *m*
shilling shilling *m*
Swiss franc franc suisse *m*
US dollar dollar américain *m*
yen yen *m*

Français	English
200FF	FF200
200£	£200
200DM	DM200
20 millions FF	FF20m
1 267 000	1,267,000
12,5	12.5